HAGOP KEVORKIAN SERIES ON NEAR EASTERN ART
AND CIVILIZATION

The publication of this work has been aided by
a grant from the Hagop Kevorkian Fund.

NABATEAN
ARCHAEOLOGY
TODAY

Avraham Negev

New York University Press · New York *and* London · *1986*

Library of Congress Cataloging-in-Publication Data
Negev, Avraham.
    Nabatean archaeology today.

    (Hagop Kevorkian series on Near Eastern art and
civilization)
    Bibliography:p.
    Includes index.
    1. Nabataeans. 2. Jordan—Antiquities. 3. Negev
(Israel)—Antiquities. 4. Sinai Peninsula (Egypt)—
Antiquities. 5. Excavations (Archaeology)—Jordan.
6. Excavations (Archaeology)—Israel—Negev.
7. Excavations (Archaeology)—Egypt—Sinai Peninsula.
8. Israel—Antiquities. 9. Egypt—Antiquities.
I. Title. I. Series.
DS154.22.N45   1986   933   86-5280
ISBN 0-8147-5760-X

To Karl Schmitt-Korte
*without whose help much of my work
could not have been accomplished.*

Nbṭ = One who digs for water.
(Medieval Arab diction-
aries).

Contents

List of Illustrations

Picture credits. Expeditions: Elusa Archaeological Expedition: 63, 64, 65, 66; Oboda Archaeological Expedition: 2, 4, 5, 6, 22, 26, 28, 60, 61; Mampsis Archaeological Expedition: 24, 27, 29, 30, 31, 32, 33, 34, 35, 39, 40, 41, 42, 43, 44, 45, 46, 47, 55, 56, 57, 58; Sinai Research Expedition: 62. Other sources: Dr. R. Cleave, aerial photographs: 23, 25; Elia Photo Service, Jerusalem: 14, 15, 20, 36; drawings by Mrs. Yael Avi-Yonah-Goldfarb: 7, 8; courtesy, Israel Museum: 59; Jaussen-Savignac, *Mission* I, pl. 1: 38; drawings by Mrs. Anat Negev-Palti: 1, 3 (after Todd in Woolley and Lawrence, fig. 59), 11, 21, 48 (after Wiegand, *Petra*). Sources that cannot be identified: 9, 10, 12, 53, 54.

Introduction

Forty years ago, in 1944 on a visit to the American School of Oriental Research in Jerusalem, Professor Nelson Glueck presented me with a small fragment of a painted Nabatean bowl and urged me to look for similar fragments. Less than a year before, I had joined a small group of volunteers who made great efforts to make the desert bloom, which was not easily done. There was no one to teach us how to cultivate the unknown land, or how to raise plants in an inhospitable desert. In despair, we turned to the ancient towns, villages, and fields that were within walking distance of our small camp. This, my first encounter with "Nabateans," "Byzantines," and the subject of ancient agriculture, was thus based purely on need. It was ten years after my first visit to the Negev that I began to pursue archaeology in a more systematic way.

Since the discovery of Petra by J. L. Burckhardt in 1812, the study of the Nabateans has virtually become the study of Petra. However, the Nabateans and Petra are not entirely identical. In reality, Petra was the result of an effort of almost a millennium during which the Nabateans became the true masters of the desert. Yet, when Petra and the Nabatean realm became part of the Roman Empire, and the Nabateans lost their share of the international spice trade, they did not vanish, as one might suppose as a consequence of studies carried out by means of modern scientific methods.

Being an Israeli researcher dealing with the Nabateans is not a simple matter. Not only are Nabatean centers like Petra in the Hashemite Kingdom of Jordan, el-Hegr-Egra (Hagra, Egra of the classical sources, is known today as el-Hegr in Saudi Arabia) in Saudi Arabia, and Seeia in Syria closed to him; he is not even wanted at a convention on Nabatean archaeology held at Oxford, England. Nevertheless, these drawbacks have positive sides. Twenty-five years of excavations in Nabatean Oboda, Mampsis, and Elusa have made it obvious that Petra, important as it is, reveals only a part of Nabatean history and archaeology. Petra was economically unimportant, and were it not for the links in the Nabatean chain of trade routes in the Negev, Petra could hardly have developed. Moreover, since I was not directly involved in work on Nabatean sites in the areas mentioned, I was gradually able to get a picture of the development of Nabatean culture in its broad outlines, uncluttered by excessive details, which often result in too narrow a perspective.

Studying the history of the Nabateans, a people who did not record their history in writing, may at first seem to be blocked by a heavy, impregnable wall. Its development differed from whatever a scholar may have experienced in researching the history of peoples whose chief basis was agriculture. This necessitated the development of new tools for research, by which every crack in this heavy wall might be breached. This study attempts to show how some of these research tools were made.

My work could not have been done without the help of numerous people. First, there were my assistants at the Hebrew University and the numerous volunteers who for over twenty years helped in collecting material. There were also friends from abroad who drew my attention to recent excavations and discoveries in different areas I cannot visit myself. I also wish to thank my friend and colleague Karl Schmitt-Korte for his faithful cooperation in Nabatean studies. It was the endless discussions with a number of scholars, students, and friends that helped me to crystallize many of the ideas expressed in this book. No less important was the help in obtaining illustrative material, which assisted in the development of Nabatean archaeology as a course at the Hebrew University.

I am, of course, especially grateful to the New York University Hagop Kevorkian Center for Near Eastern Studies and its staff for inviting me to deliver these lectures and to submit the manuscript for publication.

Avraham Negev
Jerusalem

History and Chronology [1]

Two major sources on which all studies of Nabatean history are based have survived from classical times. The first is Diodorus of Sicily's account of the campaign of Antigonus Monophtalmos against the Nabateans in 312 B.C.E., which with all probability was based on the observations of an eyewitness, Hieronymus of Cardia. The second source is Strabo, who based his writings on both earlier and contemporary sources. It is unlikely, however, that Strabo visited Petra or any other part of the Nabatean realm.

Let us turn first to the earlier source. Research on the Diodorus-Hieronymus account has made much progress since Dalman's researches were published.[2] For Dalman, Diodorus was just a "babbler." Abel first pointed out the importance of this source,[3] though Jane Hornblower was the first to give it full credit. In fact, she used Diodorus's references to the Nabateans in her recent book as a means of proving the authenticity of these and other chapters—copied by Diodorus—as part of Hieronymus's original work, which has not been preserved.[4] Several points in the Diodorus-Hieronymus account have either been totally overlooked or have not been given proper attention.

Nabatean history officially began in 312 B.C.E. (or slightly earlier). That this is far from the truth, however, becomes obvious upon a careful reading of Diodorus's description of the Nabateans: "Some of them raise camels, others sheep, pasturing them in the desert. While there are many other tribes who use the desert as pasture, the Nabateans far surpass the others in wealth although they are not much more than ten thousand in number; for not a few of them are accustomed to bring down to the sea frankincense and myrrh and the most valuable kinds of spices, which they procure from those who convey them from what is called Arabia Eudaemon."[5] To this should be added their exploitation of the asphalt of the Dead Sea, which also provided part of the Nabateans' revenues (II.48.6–9; XIX.98.1–100.1). All this implies that in 312 B.C.E. the Nabateans already had a long history during which they established trade routes running from northern Arabia to harbors on the southwestern Mediterranean coast of Palestine. The other occupation of the Nabateans, the raising of sheep and camels (which Diodorus rates as first in importance), implies that not only these trade routes were in their possession but that large stretches of pastureland were also. Moreover, a diplomatic letter that a Nabatean official wrote to Antigonus was written in "Syrian letters" (XIX.96.1). "Syrian" in this context is no doubt Aramaic, the official language of the Persian Empire, which again puts the beginning of Nabatean history earlier, sometime in the Persian period. In fact, Diodorus-Hieronymus provides the clue to Nabatean antiquity in the eighth and seventh cen-

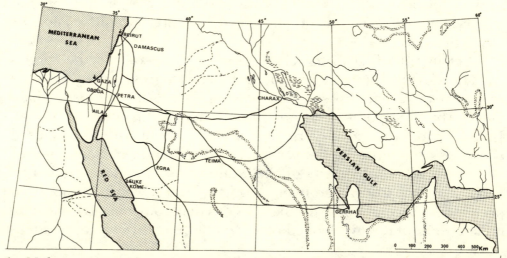

1. Nabatean caravan routes in the Middle East. (Anat Negev-Palti).

2

turies B.C.E. in a passage that was once treated as pure fiction: "Consequently neither the Assyrians of old, nor the kings of the Medes and Persians, nor yet those of the Macedonians have been able to enslave them, and although they led many great forces against them, they never brought their attempts to a successful conclusion" (II.48.5).

In earlier years, I must admit that I treated this passage as being wholly fictitious; I now think quite differently. By the fourth century B.C.E., as we have seen, the Nabateans were a well-organized group, a tribe, or a group of tribes. What singled out this group, quite certainly nomadic at this stage (see XIX.94.2–3), was its ability to procure drinking water in the desert.

Should anyone be asked to give a more comprehensive description of the cisterns dug by the Nabateans in the "waterless region," that is, the region that has no permanent sources of water, no one could have done it better than Diodorus-Hieronymus (see II.48.2–3; XIX.94.6–7). As an eyewitness (XIX.100.1), it was only Hieronymus who was able to furnish such an excellent description of this kind, and it was the Nabateans' ingenuity that prompted him to say that they were superior to the other Arabian tribes. But, as he visited only some of the areas in which they roamed, he had no way of knowing in what ways the Nabateans differed from other Arabian tribes. The main difference between the Ἐρημοσ and Ἀνυδρος lands over which the Nabateans ranged (II.48.1) is that though it rains only sporadically in the desert, the first-named region possesses some permanent sources of water. In the second-named region, the "waterless region," though there is little rainfall, it does rain regularly throughout the rainy season, which extends from October or November to March or April. Nomadic desert tribes usually depend on the few permanent sources of water, the famous oases. Consequently, these tribes, which gain their livelihood from pastureland, wander in concentric circles. The radius of their path depends both on their ability to carry drinking water and on their flocks' ability to withstand thirst. Control of the oases has frequently caused tribal feuds. Since these truly nomadic peoples never reached the stage of producing water-storage containers of any kind, they were completely dependent on natural sources. (Until recently this applied to the Bedouins, who depended either on cisterns made by their predecessors in antiquity or on wells dug by the Turkish or British governments in Palestine.) The Nabateans, who in remote antiquity undoubtedly shared the desert regions with the other Arabian nomadic

3

tribes, would certainly have known from observation that even the most desolate desert enjoys a certain amount of rainfall. The rain may not fall every year, and certainly not in a specific month, but when it does fall, there is enough water to fill natural or man-made water containers.

The words by which the Diodorus-Hieronymus account describes Nabatean cisterns could also have applied to structures of this kind found only in the deserts of Palestine or southern Arabia: "For in the waterless region, as it is called, they have dug wells at convenient intervals and have kept the knowledge of them from the people of all other nations, and so they retreat in a body into this

2. A Nabatean cistern in the vicinity of Oboda.

4

region out of danger. For since they themselves know about the places of hidden water and open them up, they have for their use drinking water in abundance" (II.48.2). In still more detail: "They take refuge in the desert, using this as a fortress; for it lacks water and cannot be crossed by others, but to them alone, since they have prepared subterranean reservoirs lined with stucco, it furnishes safety. As the earth in some places is clayey and in others is of soft stone, they make great excavations in it, the mouths of which they make very small, but by constantly increasing the width as they dig deeper, they finally make them of such size that each side has a length of one plethrum [about 100 feet]. After filling these reservoirs with rain water, they close the openings, making them even with the rest of the ground, and they leave signs that are known to themselves but are unrecognizable by others. They water their flocks [λεῖα in the text, translated by Geer by "cattle," which is a mistake in this context] every other day, so that, if they flee [or, rather, wander] through waterless places, they may not need a continuous supply of water" (XIX.94.6–9).

Except for the size of the reservoirs, which were much larger, this description fits to the last detail the numerous Nabatean cisterns that may still be seen in the Negev. Nabatean cisterns of the fourth century B.C.E. were far more sophisticated than the plastered cisterns of the Iron Age, which are found throughout the Holy Land. The ability to produce a perfect cube (the shape of a Nabatean cistern) with corners that form perfect right angles, and to construct a perfectly made stone support pillar with accurately spaced, combed, oblique stone dressing composed of water-resistant plaster of unmatched quality, must have developed over the course of hundreds of years.

On this matter we have to enter into the sphere of speculation. The easiest way to explain this astounding phenomenon is to ascribe it to a process of development for which the Nabateans were responsible. This would mean that the perfect reservoirs of the late Persian period mentioned by Diodorus-Hieronymus were developed by the Nabateans during the times of the Babylonians or even the Assyrians, to whose times the origin of the Nabateans is ascribed by Diodorus-Hieronymus. Another possibility is to consider the Nabateans to have been good disciples of the people of southern Arabia, who made sophisticated waterworks during the Iron Age. But even if this latter were the case, it would have needed people sufficiently

5

knowledgeable to be able to absorb the necessary knowledge, which would again put the Nabateans on a level much higher than that of the other northern Arabian tribes. In any case, the relation of the Nabateans to the other southern cultures has not yet been sufficiently investigated, and these cultures are themselves still very little known.

In the past few years I have tried hard to deal with the problem of the antiquity of the Nabateans from a completely new angle. Beginning in 1956, when the Israeli army first conquered Sinai, scores of photographs of Sinaitic inscriptions had been piling up on my desk. This number increased to many hundreds following the conquest of Sinai in 1967. I have visited the region several times, and in 1971 I spent the last week of the year photographing hundreds of inscriptions at the pilgrims' halt at Wadi Haggag.[6]

Since they were discovered, the Nabatean graffiti have aroused little scholarly interest, in great part because they consist mostly of personal names and short invocations; too, since few of them were dated, they have been considered to have very little historical interest.[7] I refused to accept the verdict unanimously passed on these inscriptions, if only because of their exceedingly large number. In CIS II 2743 Sinaitic-Nabatean graffiti were published (less than 500 Nabatean inscriptions come from all other regions!). Since I began to work on these inscriptions, the number of recorded Nabatean inscriptions in Sinai has risen to between 3,500 and 4,000. This is a very large number, which I could not dismiss as unimportant or uninteresting. The first problem with which I tried to cope with the aid of this material was its relation to the region in which it was found. I shall return to this point in Chapter IV. Once I completed the general list in my PNNR, I began to prepare analytical tables. Some of these tables deal with the history of personal names in each of the four major Nabatean regions: northern Arabia (NA), mainly Egra; Edom and Moab (EM), mainly Petra; the Hauran (H); and Sinai, which includes personal names of the central Negev and Wadi Tumeilat in Egypt but are mainly from southern Sinai (SEN). The general list now includes 1,249 personal names.[8] Of these, 360 personal names occur in NA only, 217 in EM only, 118 in the H only, and 331 in the Sinai only. A mere 24 personal names are common to all four regions, including the royal names Aretas, Malichus, Rabel, and Huldu. Some of the names common to all regions are much more frequent in Sinai than in any other region. One of

6

these names is ʾAusos, which is mentioned 241 times in Sinai as against 9 times in NA, 3 times in EM, and 4 times in the H. Forty-five personal names are three-region names, and 129 names are two-region names. Some of these are Sinaitic personal names that penetrated other regions. Thus, the name Walu occurs 409 times in Sinai but only 8 times in NA and 16 times in EM; the name Kalbu occurs 134 times in Sinai but only once in both NA and EM. (Kalbu, meaning "dog" in the Semitic languages, is of intrinsic interest. Dogs are abhorred by Arabs, and no Arabian would give his son that name unless it also had a different meaning. In my analytical research I found that an important group of personal names derives from celestial bodies and that Kalbu may be derived from Sirius, which is so important for orientation in the desert.) Of the two-region names, the name ʿAmmayu occurs 289 times in Sinai and only once in NA. Personal names like these may certainly be considered as properly Sinaitic. I believe that the division of personal names into separate regional names contains a clue to the antiquity of the Nabateans.

A question that has never been properly answered is: Who were the Nabateans—an ethnic group, a tribe, a group of tribes? Without written history, this question may not be answered directly. As noted earlier, Diodorus-Hieronymus states that though many Arabian tribes used the desert as pasture, the Nabateans were wealthier than the other tribes. Diodorus-Hieronymus refers to the Nabateans as an Arabian tribe. Arabian tribes usually have both tribal and proper names of their own, and a member of a tribe is usually designated by the word *benei* or *bani*, "sons of." The Nabatean vocabulary includes very few tribal references. In contrast, the contemporary and slightly later Palmyrene inscriptions abound with such references.[9] All contributions and donations made by members of the Palmyrene upper class toward the construction of public buildings include a reference to both the contributor's father's and grandfather's names as well as to the name of the tribe, always preceded by the word *benei*. Contemporary and slightly later Safaitic and Thamudic inscriptions, which abound in northern Arabia, southern and eastern Edom, and the Hauran—the same regions in which Nabatean inscriptions abound—also include tribal references.[10] In my opinion, this fact may be interpreted in one of two ways: it may indicate that the Nabateans never had such a tribal social structure, which does not seem very likely, or it may hint at the remote antiquity of the Nabateans.

7

Very few Nabatean inscriptions pertain to the second and first centuries B.C.E. The Nabatean inscriptions of Egra in NA are from 1 to 75 C.E., which are also the approximate dates of the Nabatean inscriptions of EM, the H, and the Negev. The Sinaitic inscriptions date from the second and third centuries C.E.[11] I suggest that all traces of tribal organization had been obliterated by the time the Nabateans began to engrave inscriptions on the rocks of southern Sinai. This may also confirm Diodorus's-Hieronymus's statement regarding the antiquity of the Nabateans. In the Assyrian and Persian period, long before the Nabateans established their hold on the distant regions of the Hauran and Sinai, they may have constituted a tribe or group of tribes, but the need to establish caravan halts along the routes leading to the Mediterranean, and later to Damascus also (at the beginning of my research I ascribed the conquest of the Hauran and Damascus to the need to compensate for the loss of Gaza to Alexander Jannaeus about 100 B.C.E. and to establish an alernative caravan route)[12] slowly caused the formation of separate Nabatean districts, which account for cultural differences; for differences in religious practices, as evidenced by theophoric personal names particular to each region; and also for the creation of other regional personal names. In many cases, the fact that some personal names are common to two or three adjoining regions may be explained by the movement of people from one region to another. On this point, the rather rare geographical personal names are instructive. Thus, in Sinai we find people named Hagru and Hagiru;[13] Hagra was the Nabatean name for the important commercial center of Egra in NA (13 people had these names). The 7 people named Zᶜabliyu[14]— Zaᶜbal is a place near Teima, another important Nabatean center in NA—belong to the same class. On the other hand, a personal name like Paran, which occurs 46 times in Sinai,[15] attests persons who were born in this most important oasis in southern Sinai, biblical Paran (e.g., Gen. 14:6), Pharan of the late Roman and early Christian sources. Only one man by this name is known from NA. Not less instructive are the few personal names based on tribal affiliations. Thus, the personal name Banun, which occurs once in NA, is more common in Safaitic (5 times).[16] Galhamu is a version of the tribe Jalham and occurs once in NA and 24 times in the Safaitic inscriptions.[17] The personal name Abishat, which occurs 7 times in the H, is found 11 times in Safaitic inscriptions and also in Greek form in the H.[18] The personal name ʾAdnun—the name of the first ancestor

8

of the southern Arabian tribes[19]—occurs once in NA and is also attested in Safaitic and Qatabanian. ʾAkiu, found 4 times in NA, is represented twice in Safaitic.[20] Qamriya occurs once in NA and 24 times in Safaitic inscriptions.[21] These may well be members of Safaitic and Thamudic tribes who joined the Nabateans. Tribal names are still rarer in Sinai. The name ʿAleidu, which occurs twice in Sinai, is close to the name Bani ʿAleideh, which is an Arab tribe in southwestern Sinai.[22] Two personal names occurring in Sinai are of special interest. Arabiu, "Arab,"[23] occurs 9 times. This name is attested in Safaitic (4 times), Thamudic (2 times), and Palmyrene (2 times) and also occurs in Greek form. The other name, (El)-Sharqiyu, occurs 3 times and also in Safaitic, Thamudic, and Minaean. In Greek it takes the form Sarakenos; Saracen is also the name of a tribe in the Sinaitic peninsula.[24] It is interesting to note that tribal personal names are more common in NA (14 names) than in Sinai (4 names) or in Sinai-EM (1 name). It was northern Arabia that swarmed with numerous tribes. It is possible that the inscriptions in which tribal names are mentioned were engraved by non-Nabatean tribesmen who lived with the Nabateans and used their language. There are several definite examples of this phenomenon, the most famous being the two inscriptions engraved by Masʿudu, king of Lihyan, found at Egra.[25]

The relative isolation and separation of each of the four major Nabatean regions may also be exemplified by the penetration of Greek and Roman names. As might be expected, the largest number of foreign personal names is found at Petra, capital of the Nabatean kingdom, at which "many Romans and many other foreigners sojourn[ed]" (Strabo, *Geography* XVI.4.21). Among the 39 Greek and Roman personal names found at Petra are Atlas, Ision, Alexa, Anaximedes, Apollonius, Archelaus, Ariston, Athenodorus, Glaucos, Gorgias, Diodorus, and Dionysus. Next comes NA with 29 foreign personal names, such as Eukleion, Euphronios, Alexios, Askides, Aspasianus, Aribas, Erastines, and Hephaistion. Most of these men were mercenaries who came to participate in fighting,[26] but Hephaistion, a chiliarch, who most likely served at Egra, was a Nabatean, as attested by his father's name, which is a good Nabatean name.[27] Aribas too was a Nabatean, whose father's name was ʿAbdobodat.[28] The H, closer to Syria, is third with only 13 foreign personal names. It is only natural that Sinai is last, with 6 personal names, some of which are rather doubtful. The name Aflasu is pos-

9

sibly Apelles and comes from Nessana in the Negev.[29] Zenobius comes from Wadi Tumeilat in eastern Egypt.[30] The name Julius comes from the same site.[31] Contrary to the other names mentioned earlier, which are rare, the name Silvanus occurs 7 times in southern Sinai, either as son or father of a man named ʿAbd-ʾalbaʿali,[32] which is a good Nabatean personal name. The name Sarafiu, which occurs 10 times, could either be the Greek-Egyptian Serapeion or the Arab Sarif.[33] Farfariu, which occurs once, comes either from Arabic *farfariu,* "sparrow," or from Porphyrius.[34] This again shows how isolated the four Nabatean regions were from each other during the Roman period.

Also of much interest in this connection are personal names based on occupation, possibly that of its holder or of his family. Thus, at Egra in NA we find ʾAkkur, meaning "gravedigger."[35] This name is appropriate at a site that housed the second-largest Nabatean necropolis. There were numerous male and female servants and slaves of different kinds named ʾAmat, ʾAphtiyu, Hana, and Zabin,[36] and again, the great variety of names for servants is appropriate for a society in which more than 60 percent of the tomb owners belonged to the upper classes.[37] On the other hand, of the 7 occupational names attested at Petra, only one is connected with servitude, which is in accord with Strabo's statement in his description of Petra: "Since they have but few slaves, they are served by their kinsfolk, for the most part, or by one another, or by themselves; so that the custom extends even to their kings" (XVI.4.26). The name Wakila means "manager," "agent," "steward."[38] The name Hamlath, mentioned twice at Egra, means "porter," "carrier." It is very common in Safaitic (39 times) but is less common in Thamudic (3 times). It well suits the most important Nabatean caravan center,[39] as may also the name Yamuru, which possibly means "to convey," "to buy."[40] The name Ghuzaiyat, "warrior,"[41] accords with the history of Egra, as do the names Redipha, "soldier in reserve,"[42] and Rami, "archer," "slinger."[43] Shigʿu, "brave,"[44] is very common in Safaitic. Finally, Shaqia, "water carrier," is relevant to both the caravan and the army.[45]

Occupational personal names are quite different in southern Sinai. We thus find that one of the most common groups of names derives from the personal name Qainu, such as ʾIbn-ʾal-Qain, ʾIbn-ʾal-Qainu, ʾIbn-ʾal-Qaini, and ʾal-Qainat, which all derive from *qain,* "smith," "artisan."[46] This name does not occur anywhere else

10

in the Nabatean realm; nor is it known in the other ancient Arabian languages. It compares with "Tubal-cain, the master of all coppersmiths and blacksmiths" (Gen. 4:22). The copper and malachite mines at Serabit el-Khadem and Wadi Mughara in Sinai are well known. Numerous Nabatean inscriptions have been found in the vicinity of the copper smelting site at Wadi Nasb. The name Waqilu, "steward," "manager," "agent,"[47] may be allied to these enterprises. This name is found at Egra (see p. 10) in the form of Waqila. Another Sinaitic name is ʾAkhrashu, ʾal-ʾAkhrasu, or Kharshu (89 times), meaning "hunter of lizards."[48] Lizards abound in Sinai and possibly served as food. In Sinai the names Zabnu and Zabni meant "slave."[49] One group of names is connected with tending herds of sheep and goats (e.g., Halibu, "milker").[50] Nashgu, and the very common diminutive Nashigu, means "weaver."[51] One of the most important names in this group is Shumraḥ (105 times), Shumraḥu (16 times), meaning a branch of a palm tree laden with dates.[52] The name Nithagu, one who helps females give birth, is rare and is found only once in Sinai and once in Safaitic.[53] In Sinai the name Naqlu, "carrier," is common in Safaitic.[54] A worker is named ʿAmlu.[55] At Egra the name Ghuzaiyat, "warrior," is Ghuzaiyatu in Sinai.[56] The name Qaiyafu means one who follows and examines someone's footprints.[57] Finally, quite common is Qashatu, "archer," not so much in the military sense of the word, but in connection with hunting.[58]

The group of theophoric personal names is the most important one by which this separation into regions may be studied. This group, the largest, numbers 252 personal names in all four regions. The largest number of theophoric personal names (94) is from Sinai. These names deserve a separate study, and only the most important ones will be mentioned here.

Eleven personal names in Sinai contain the element *baʿal*. Among these are ʾUshbaʿal, ʾUshbaʿali, ʾUsh-ʾalbaʿali, meaning "gift of Baʿal";[59] Garmʾalbaʿali (156 times), Garmʾalbaʿaliyu, "Baʿal has decided";[60] Zaidʾalbaʿali, "Baʿal has increased";[61] ʿAbdʾalba ʿali, "servant of Baʿal";[62] Shamsh-ʾalbaʿali, "god Shamas is my Baʿal"; Sa(ʿa)d-ʾalbaʿali, "Baʿal is my helper";[63] Thaimʾ-albaʿali, "servant of Baʿal."[64] None of these composite names occurs in any other ancient Arabian language. From Petra comes one Baʿal-matan, "Baʿal is firm."[65] Baʿal does not figure at all in two- and three-region names. Thus, Baʿal is a local Sinaitic deity.

Another important deity is ʾAllah, or ʾIllah,[66] forming the theophoric element of numerous personal names. We thus find in Sinai ʾAushʾallah, "god's faith," "god's covenant," "god's wrath"[67] (found also in the Greek forms Ausalla, Ausallos).[68] Although it is a Sinaitic name (49 times), ʾAushʾallahi occurs also in NA once and at Petra 3 times.[69] In this group one woman, ʾAmat-ʾallahi, "she-servant of ʾAllahi," is represented.[70] Other names with the component ʾAllah are Garm-ʾallah, Garm-ʾallahi (51 times), "ʾAllah decided"[71] (Garamelos in Greek form);[72] Hab-ʾallahi, "beloved by ʾAllah";[73] and Han-ʾallahi, "ʾAllahi is gracious."[74] This last-mentioned name, occurring only once in Sinai, is a common Safaitic personal name.[75] (Annelos in the Greek form).[76] Still other names are Maʿan-ʾallah,[77] Mʿan-ʾallah, "apparently ʾAllah replied";[78] ʿAb-ʾallahi,[79] possibly a contraction of ʿAbd-ʾallahi, "servant of ʾAllahi"; Sad-ʾallahi,[80] possibly a contraction of Sa ʿad-ʾallahi, "ʾAllahi is a good omen"; Shakem-ʾallahi,[81] "ʾAllahi rewards"; and Shalm-lahi,[82] "ʾAllahi is peace."[83] These personal names, quite common in Sinai, also penetrated NA. We thus find the name ʾAhsh-ʾallahi,[84] "he whom ʾAllah knows," and Tham-ʾallahi,[85] "servant of ʾAllah."

In EM personal names with the ʾAllah component occur more often. We thus find the rare name ʿAba-ʾallahi,[86] "ʾAllahi is eternal";[87] ʾAmar-ʾallahi,[88] "servant of ʾAllah";[89] Hani-ʾallahi,[90] "servant of ʾAllah" (Anaelos in Greek form);[91] Zar-ʾallahi,[92] the meaning of which is not clear; Halaf-(ʾa)llahi,[93] "ʾAllah's successor" (Alafallos in Greek);[94] Q(o)s-ʾallah,[95] perhaps the Edomite god Qos, meaning "Qos is ʾAllah"; Sabʿa-ʾallahi,[96] "ʾAllah is a lion," is common in Safaitic[97] and close to the Hebrew Ariel;[98] Sai-ʾallahi,[99] "ʾAllah assists";[100] and Shakr-ʾallahi,[101] "ʾAllah praises."[102]

ʾAllahi forms personal names, two of which are common also in adjoining regions of the Nabatean realm. The personal name Wahab-ʾallahi (10 times in NA, 26 in Sinai, 9 in EM, and 2 in the H) is common in all four regions.[103] The name means "gift of ʾAllahi."[104] It is found in various forms in Greek (e.g., Ouabelos).[105] Found in three adjoining regions is the name Saʿad-ʾallahi (8 times in NA, 117 in Sinai, 4 in EM, and 2 in the H);[106] the name means "ʾAllahi is a good omen" (see above for the Sinaitic form of this name). In the form of Saʿad-lahi, which is a shortened form, this name is found 3 times in NA, 11 times in Sinai, and once in the H.[107] Other three-region names are ʾAush-ʾallahi (once in NA, 49 times in Sinai, and 3 times in EM).[108] In the shortened form, ʾAush-ʾalla, it is found

12

only in Sinai; ʿAbd-ʾallahi, "servant of ʾAllahi" (2 times in NA, 38 in Sinai, and 8 in EM);[109] Thaim-ʾallahi, "servant of ʾAllahi" (4 times in NA, 64 in Sinai, and 4 in EM).[110] It is found in various forms in Greek (Thaimalas, Themalles, Themellas).[111] The name Ḥalaf-ʾallahi (4 times in NA and 3 in EM)[112] is found in the shortened form of Ḥalaf-lahi in EM only. Thus, unlike Baʿal, which is Sinaitic only, the element ʾAllahi is a component of personal names in all four Nabatean regions.

Another ancient god, ʾEl, was once the chief god of the Semites.[113] It formed a component of a great variety of personal names. In northern Arabia, Dani-ʾel, "ʾEl recompensed," is found once only;[114] it is also rare in Safaitic and Thamudic,[115] and is perhaps a borrowing from the Hebrew.[116] Wadad-l-ʾel, "friend, lover of ʾEl,"[117] found only once in northern Arabia, is very common in Lihyanic, Safaitic, Thamudic, Minaean (10 times), and Qatabanian (18 times)[118] and must have spread from southern Arabia northward. This name occurs also in the Greek form of Ouyaddelos.[119] Also found once in northern Arabia are the names: Waqi-ha-ʾel, "ʾEl protects,"[120] which occurs 3 times in Safaitic;[121] Mir-ʾel, "ʾEl provides,"[122] which occurs 3 times in Safaitic;[123] ʾEl-ʾaz, "ʾEl is powerful,"[124] which is also found in Himyarite, Minaean (5 times), and Sabaean;[125] and ʿAli-ʾel, "ʾEl is eminent,"[126] which is found twice in Qatabanian.[127] Rabib-ʾel, "ʾEl is master,"[128] is found 5 times in northern Arabia and also 5 times in Safaitic, as well as in Thamudic and Sabaean.[129]

In Sinai, ʾAmar-ʾel, "servant of ʾEl,"[130] is found once but is found 20 times in Safaitic and 6 times in Thamudic[131] (Amrilios in Greek);[132] Garam-ʾel, "ʾEl's covenant, anger, or faith,"[133] is found 2 times in Sinai and 190 times in Safaitic[134] (Garamelos in Greek form);[135] Hai-ʾel, "ʾEl lives,"[136] is found twice in Sinai, 18 times in Safaitic, and once in Minaean and Sabaean.[137] (Compare the Hebrew name Hiel [1 Kings 16:34]); ʿAbd-ʾel, "servant of ʾEl,"[138] is found 3 times in Sinai, 30 times in Safaitic, 2 times in Thamudic, and 4 times in Qatabanian[139] (Abdelos in Greek form);[140] ʿAzaz-ʾel, "ʾEl is mighty,"[141] comes from eastern Egypt. It is attested twice in Qatabanian.[142] (Compare with Hebrew Azazel [Lev. 16:8].) ʾAmar-ʾel, "ʾEl is life,"[143] is found once in Sinai and 5 times in Safaitic, 3 times in Thamudic, and once in Sabaean;[144] Falat-ʾel, "ʾEl delivered,"[145] comes from eastern Egypt and is found 9 times in Safaitic;[146] Qasham-ʾel, or Qasam-ʾel, meaning uncertain,[147] is found once in Sinai, Lihyanite, Safaitic, and Qatabanian.[148]

In Edom and Moab, Hur-ʾel,[149] is found once and also once in Safaitic,[150] and is doubtfully theophoric. The other name is Natir-ʾel, meaning "ʾEl protects."[151] There is no connection between these names and the personal names of the other Arabian languages.

In the Hauran, Han-ʾel, "ʾEl is gracious,"[152] is found 6 times (Annelos, Anelos in Greek form);[153] Taʿa-ʾel, "ʾEl is obedient,"[154] is found once in the H and twice in Safaitic;[155] Natir-ʾel which means also "ʾEl watches"[156] and Z̧aʿad-ʾel, "ʾEl mounts,"[157] which are found twice in the H and 7 times in Safaitic;[158] Shaiʿa-ʾel, "ʾEl accompanies,"[159] is found once in the H and 31 times in Safaitic;[160] Shakr-ʾel, "ʾEl is praised,"[161] is found once in the H and 24 times in Safaitic (Sachrelos in Greek form).[162]

The only name containing the ʾEl element in all four Nabatean regions is Rav-ʾel, "ʾEl is great," the name of two Nabatean kings (never of ordinary men).[163] Yet, it is one of the most frequent Arabian personal names: it occurs 108 times in Safaitic, twice in Thamudic, once in Himyarite, once in Qatabanian, 10 times in Sabaean,[164] and 10 times in Palmyrene[165] (Rabbelos in Greek form).[166] It also formed the name ʿAbd-rabʾel, "servant of Rabel," found in NA, EM, and the H.[167] Ram-ʾel, "ʾEl is exalted," is a three-region name and is found 6 times in NA and once in Sinai and the H.[168] It is found in Safaitic 6 times[169] and also 6 times in Palmyrene.[170]

ʾAllah and ʾEl are common Semitic deities, and the presence of these elements in personal names in all four Nabatean regions, although not with the same frequency, may point to an ancient common origin of the Nabateans.

Let us consider other important deities.[171] Dushara, the Nabatean supreme god, is represented twice by two personal names only—by ʿAbd-Dushara, "slave of Dushara,"[172] and by Tym-dushara, "servant of Dushara," The second name occurs once in NA, 6 times in Sinai, and 2 times in the H[173] (Theimadousarous in Greek form).[174]

ʾAllat was the chief goddess. In Sinai, Tym-ʾallat, "servant of ʾAllat,"[175] is found once and is also attested 5 times in Qatabanian, 3 times in Sabaean,[176] and in Palmyrene,[177] (Themallathos in Greek form);[178] Temalat, the shortened form, occurs once in Sinai[179] and twice in Safaitic.[180] In NA, Suhai-lat, "ʾAllat excels,"[181] occurs once and is found 7 times in Safaitic.[182]

In Edom and Moab, Malik-ʾallatu, "King of ʾAllat,"[183] is found once, 11 times in Safaitic, and once in Thamudic;[184] Shalm-ʾallat, "peace of ʾAllat," occurs once[185] (Sal(a)mallathos in Greek form)[186] and once also in both Qatabanian and Sabaean;[187] Shaqilat, which should perhaps be emended to Shaqi-ʾallat, "ʾAllat is exalted,"[188] is the name of two Nabatean queens, and is found in Safaitic twice.[189]

ʾAllat, as a four-region name, appears as Waʾilat, which perhaps should be Waʾil-ʾallat, "ʾAllat is my refuge," is found 3 times in NA, 20 times in Sinai, and once in EM and the H;[190] it is found in most other Arabian languages: Lihyanite (once), Safaitic (16 times), Thamudic (4 times), Minaean (twice), and Sabaean (once).[191] As a two-region name, ʾAllat is found in EM and the H as Wahab-ʾallat, "gift of ʾAllat."[192] As Palmyrene name it occurs 108 times,[193] once in Himyarite, and 3 times in Qatabanian[194] (Ouaballathos in Greek form).[195]

Finally, numerous minor gods and goddesses may be considered. Manutu[196] is found in EM as Wahab-manutu, "gift of Manutu";[197] in NA as Zaid-manutu, "Manutu augments"[198] (twice); and as ʿAbd-manutu, "servant of Manutu,"[199] and also in Lihyanite (once) and Thamudic;[200] ʿAbd-manuti,[201] possibly a different form of Manutu, and Taim-manutu, "servant of Manutu,"[202] are also found in NA.

ʾAl-ʿUzza[203] occurs in Sinai as ʿAbd-al-ʿazi, perhaps "servant of ʾal-ʿUzza."[204]

ʾEl-Ge[205] occurs in Sinai as ʿAbd-ʾal-go, "servant of Go," a different form of ʾEl-Ge (?),[206] and in the H as ʾAmat-ʾel-ge, "woman servant of Ge."[207] As a three-region name (NA, Sinai, and EM), it is found as ʿAbd-ʾel-ge, "servant of Ge," once in NA, 15 times in Sinai, and 3 times in EM[208] (frequently, in Greek, as Abdalgos, Abdallgas, and Abdalgou).[209]

Qaumu[210] is found in Sinai as Zaid-qaum, "Qaum augments,"[211] twice and in Safaitic once ([Zaido]kimas in Greek form);[212] ʿAbd-qaumu, "servant of Qaumu,"[213] is found once in Sinai and as ʿAbd-qaumi, a different form (diminutive?) of the former.[214]

Isis[215] is found in EM as ʾAmat-ʾIsi, "servant of Isis," once;[216] in the H as Asdoulos, "slave of Isis" (Greek name, Isidoulos, in Nabatean form [?]);[217] and in NA and EM as ʿAbd-ʾIsi, "servant of Isis."[218]

Gada ("Tyche," "Fortune")[219] is found in the H as Gadu;[220] in NA and EM as Gad-tab, "Fortune is good";[221] and in NA, Sinai, and EM as Gaddu, "Fortune," 4 and 3 times[222] (Gados, Gadiou in Greek form);[223] and 31 times in Safaitic, 3 in Thamudic,[224] and 9 in Palmyrene.[225]

Ya‘ut[226] is found in Sinai and EM as ’Amra-ya‘ut, possibly "servant of Ya‘ut,"[227] and as Yat‘u.[228] It is found in the H as Taim-yat‘u, "servant of Yat‘u," Yuthai.[229]

Mudu (doubtful)[230] is found in EM as ‘Abd-mudu, "servant of Mudu,"[231] and in the H as Rab-mudu, "Mudu is great."[232]

Mannu, "graciousness" (doubtful)[233] is found in NA as ‘Abd-mannu, "servant of Mannu."[234]

Qos[235] occurs in NA as Qos-natan, "Qos has given"[236] (Kosnatanos in Greek form),[237] and in Sinai as Qos-‘eder, "Qos is bold," 3 times[238] (Kosadaros in Greek form).[239] (See also under ’Allahi, p. 12.)

Taim-’al-Kutba, goddess of writing, appears 5 times in EM.[240]

’El-Katriu, the name of an idol venerated by the tribes of Jadis and Thasm, is found 4 times in Sinai[241] and 27 times in Safaitic.[242]

In addition to the properly theophoric names, one sometimes finds personal names based on offices that their bearers performed in service of the gods and temples. Thus, in Sinai ’el-Kahanu, "priest,"[243] is found 7 times and also in Safaitic (twice);[244] Mobakra, Mobakeru, ’Almobakeru, priest in charge of sacrifices or of the administration of the temple, occurs 114 times[245] (Almobakkerou in Greek form);[246] Kamara, "priest" appears once[247] and twice in Safaitic[248] and Palmyrene[249] (Kamareus, Kamaros in Greek form).[250]

People born during religious festivals in Sinai were given one of several names: Baḥaga, "[born] during the pilgrimage," "pilgrim," is found 38 times[251] and 6 times in Safaitic;[252] Ḥaggu, "hajj" (pilgrim), "born during the pilgrimage," appears 9 times in Sinai,[253] 75 times in Safaitic, once in Minaean,[254] and twice in Palmyrene[255] (Chagos in Greek form).[256]

An analysis of the theophoric names points to a common origin of the Nabateans, who, like the other Semites, venerated ’Allahi and ’El. The differences in the frequency in each of the four Nabatean regions may be explained, at least in part, by the number of inscriptions discovered in each region. In Sinai the Nabateans seem to have venerated mostly Ba‘al, a cult that did not penetrate the other regions, at least not as a name-forming element, and the single mention of Rakhimba‘al in Edom and Moab is instructive. It is, however, difficult to explain the fact that so few people used the name Dushara, the Nabateans' supreme god, as a component of personal names.

16

To this point, I have analyzed Nabatean personal names in support of my assumption that if indeed the Nabateans migrated from a common place of origin, generally assumed to be Arabia, they must have done so at a quite early time for this divergence into regional personal names to have developed. It may, however, also point to another possibility, namely that there never was such a migration and that in each of the four regions the people whom we call Nabateans formed the autochthonic population who were subdued by a small but very strong new element, coming from Arabia, the real Nabateans, the traces of which are very difficult to detect.

That the people who used the personal names we call Nabatean were indeed Nabateans, differing from the other Arabian peoples, we may gather from the analytical tables (CXVIII–CLI in my PNNR). Four hundred and thirty-nine personal names, constituting about one-third of the total, are specifically Nabatean personal names unknown in any other Arabian language. In addition to these, 70 personal names are very frequent in Nabatean but are of limited frequency in Safaitic and Thamudic, southern Arabia, or Palmyra. Possibly 358 personal names, less than one-third, are of non-Nabatean origin. Most are Safaitic and Thamudic; some are southern Arabian; and personal names of Palmyrene origin are still less frequent. Possibly only about 200 personal names are of common Semitic origin. This again shows that the Nabateans were an easily identifiable ethnic group until the end of the third century c.e.

Archaeology offers very few finds that substantiate the presence of Nabateans east or west of the Arabah. The scanty evidence was presented while I was studying the chronology of the Middle Nabatean period.[257] The only firm shreds of such evidence are the Early Nabatean inscription of Elusa, dated to 168 b.c.e., and of Petra, dated to the end of the second and the beginning of the first century b.c.e.[258] In addition to these inscriptions, coins and pottery sherds of the late fourth and the early first century b.c.e. were found at Petra and on three sites in the Negev. We may connect these finds with the Nabateans only by circumstantial evidence, according to which they occupied Petra and the Negev in the Hellenistic period (i.e., the Early Nabatean period). Attempts to discover houses built by the Nabateans in the Hellenistic period failed. In the excavations recently made at Moyet Awad, the so-called Moa in the Arabah, an important station on the Petra–Gaza road, another attempt was made by R. Cohen to locate a Hellenistic level of occupation. However, at

17

3. Elusa. A Nabatean inscription of 168 C.E.: "This [holy?] place which made Notairu for the life of Aretas, king of the Nabateans." Drawing by Mrs. Anat Negev-Palti (after Woolley and Lawrence).

this level the finds consisted only of coins and pottery, above which a caravansery was built in the Middle Nabatean period.[259]

In fact, it is again the Diodorus-Hieronymus account that helps to solve this riddle. This source reveals that in this Early period the Nabateans were, like the other Arabian desert tribes, tent dwellers. At one point it reads: "There are also other tribes of Arabs, some of whom even till the soil, mingling with the tribute-paying peoples,

18

4. Oboda. A Rhodian stamped jar handle of the second century B.C.E. found in a crevice in the rock formation on the acropolis. It reads· "In the time of Damokles. [In the month of] Agrianios."

5. Oboda. A "Megarian" bowl of the Hellenistic period. (A. Chai).

and have the same customs as the Syrians, except that they do not dwell in houses" (XIX.94.10). On speaking specifically of the Nabateans, the Diodorus-Hieronymus account says: "It is their custom neither to sow corn, plant fruit-bearing trees, use wine, nor construct any houses; and if anyone is found acting contrary to this, death is his penalty. They follow this custom because they believe that those who possess these things are, in order to retain the use of them, easily compelled by the powerful to do their bidding" (XIX.94.3–4). Diodorus-Hieronymus apparently took it for granted that the Nabateans, like the other nomads, lived in tents and did not find it necessary to mention this fact.

In the early stages of my researches, I told my students that a system must be found by which ancient encampments could be located. Since I had lived in the desert from my early youth, I was well acquainted with the Bedouins' encampments. I observed them pitching their tents and also when leaving their encampments for their annual wanderings, either from the winter house to the summer house, which might be a matter of moving from one side of the hill to the other, or, in cases of insufficient pasture, to more distant regions. When they leave a camp, it is mostly perishables that they leave behind: a broken wooden peg, a piece of rope, a broken waterskin, and similar useless objects. As time goes on, after a few rainy seasons, these slowly decay. The remains of pottery means little. The Bedouins never produced pottery; their water jars and large dough mixing bowls were produced in Gaza and Hebron and were bought in the weekly markets at Beersheba. From the early Islamic period these were fired black, with a very limited range of decoration; this has not changed much since and is thus of very little help in dating. It is only chance finds that may be of some help. Bedouin women cover their faces with strings of coins, ranging from coins of the Second Temple period to coins of modern times; mostly they use coins that are no longer in use. Thus, in the period of the British Mandate over Palestine, Turkish and Egyptian copper and silver constituted the bulk of the coins used for adornment (women of well-to-do Bedouin families often used the silver talers of Maria Theresa). Nevertheless, coins provide some chronological pegs. Moreover, out of necessity Bedouins often resorted to robbery. In earlier times robbery was institutionalized in the form of annual raids on towns and villages, which were an important source of nonperishable materials that may be found in Bedouin encampments. Dur-

20

ing World War II the Bedouins used metal canisters marked "USA" to transport water more often they used black clay jars; after 1948 these canisters were replaced by plastic cans bearing the initials of the Israel Defence Army (ZHL). Bottles from Spinney's supply company (in British times) and bottles made by Israeli glass factories, along with empty cans round out the leavings found in deserted Bedouin encampments. I was convinced that by carefully studying remains of this kind, one could work his way back and be able to identify encampments of the Byzantine, Roman, Hellenistic, and even earlier periods.

By a stroke of luck the process was much shortened. In the summer of 1975 I returned to Oboda for a short period of excavations. One of the goals of this season's work was to locate Nabatean tombs. While surveying the northeastern fringes of the site I came upon a large number of upright standing stelae, which I thought were tombstones. Indeed, pottery sherds of the Middle Nabatean period were scattered around the stelae. After clearing away a thin layer of topsoil, however, we hit upon the natural rock. Since the object of our work was to locate tombs, we abandoned the site with-

6. Oboda. A campsite of the Middle Nabatean period.

out giving it further thought. The following year we returned to excavate the area around the Nabatean military camp.[260] East of it were the unearthed remains of a flimsily made large building, of a series of cubicles, and of a large court, all with earthen floors. The pottery found in it was also of the Middle Nabatean period, to which the military camp also belongs. While cleaning the floor of one of the rooms of the large building we came upon a large blackened half circle that contained Hellenistic pottery. The walls adjoining this half circle penetrated it, and when the floor on the opposite side of the wall was cleaned, the other half of the rounded black spot was discovered. This, we reasoned, must have been a large fireplace, perhaps of an Early Nabatean encampment.

In 1979 I came back to Elusa to continue a survey begun in 1973.[261] Some two kilometers east of the center of Elusa, along one of the roads leading to the site, I observed the remains of a deserted Bedouin encampment. I stopped to examine it and went on toward the site by foot. On the way I noted a piece of land strewn with Middle Nabatean pottery and with blackened stones. While carefully examining the ground I noticed that where the terrain was heavily strewn with pottery it was trodden and had little vegetation. An examination of these areas revealed fieldstones and large wadi pebbles blackened by fire. There was no building in the vicinity from which these stones could have been transported; thus, they had been brought to this sand-covered terrain from some distance. The remains were those of fireplaces, which were quite certainly traces of a large encampment of the Middle Nabatean period.

This discovery helped to solve the riddle of the stelae found at Oboda. As is my habit, I imparted these observations to my senior students. One of them, Uzi Avner, was occupied at that time in a survey of Biq‘at ‘Uvda northwest of Eilat, in the area at which a road leading to a new airfield was planned. On finding stelae similar to those at Oboda, he consulted me by phone. As a result of my advice, he discovered traces of the plots of the tents, and of stelae (with all probability house shrines) facing a range of hills against which the large encampment leaned. Since it is now certain that the Nabateans in the Early and Middle Nabatean periods lived in tents, it becomes obvious why it is very difficult to discover sites of the Early and Middle Nabatean periods.

In my earlier studies I had assigned the end of the Early Nabatean period to the beginning of the first century B.C.E., attributing

22

it to the conquest of Gaza by Alexander Jannaeus.[262] The chronology of the Middle Nabatean period is much simpler to reconstruct because of the wealth of ceramic, numismatic, and architectural material, not to speak of the numerous inscriptions pertaining to this period, that is available.

The basis of this chronology, which I developed for my work in the Nabatean Negev, is the accurate dating of Nabatean pottery. This was made possible by the discovery of a Nabatean potter's

7. Oboda. A Nabatean painted bowl of the first half of the first century C.E., found in the potter's workshop. Drawing by Mrs. Yael Avi-Yonah-Goldfarb.

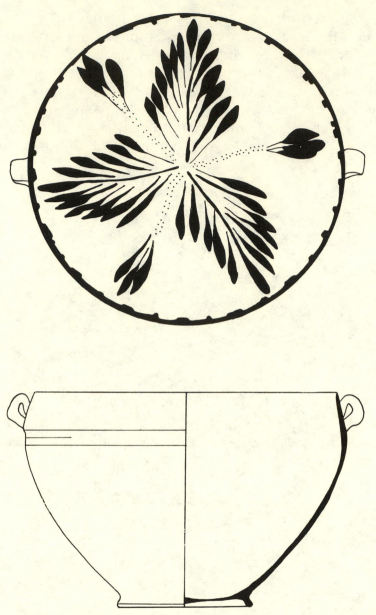

8. Oboda. A Nabatean painted cup found in the potter's workshop. Drawing by Mrs. Yael Avi-Yonah-Goldfarb.

workshop at Oboda.[263] The dating of the pottery of Oboda was confirmed by the results of the excavations of the Nabatean temple at Diban[264] and basically was not affected by Peter Parr's excavations at Petra.[265] No comparable evidence for the dating of Nabatean pottery has been produced for more than twenty years. At Oboda this pottery was dated to the years between 25 B.C.E. and 50 C.E. The earlier date was based on the presence of Augustan lamps, the so-called Herodian lamps, and of pottery of the terra sigillata type imported from Italy. The later date was determined by epigraphic evidence, the evidence of coins, and general historical considerations. The ending of the Nabatean settlement of the Middle Nabatean period at Oboda was ascribed to the arrival of new Arab tribes who wreaked havoc there. The only change in this chronology that I would introduce now would be to change the first date to 30 B.C.E., the beginning of the reign of Obodas II, when the earliest Nabatean temples were also built. The excavations at Mampsis generally confirmed this dating, but some doubt about the date of the beginning of the decline of Nabatean painted pottery has arisen, and for this reason the later date of the Middle Nabatean period was changed to 50/70 C.E.[266]

I was very disappointed when no serious attempt was made in other researches to support or disprove the suggested chronology.[267] Thus, I looked for a way to verify this chronology myself, which led me to the funerary monuments at Egra.[268] Following are some of the military implications[269] of my analysis of this study. During the first quarter of the first century C.E., Egra was com-

9. Egra. Tombs in one of the rock formations in the Nabatean necropolis.

25

10. Egra. One of the funerary inscriptions found at the necropolis (27 C.E.): "This is the tomb made by Arwas son of Farwan for himself and for Farwan his father, hipparch, and for his wife Qainu and Ḥatibat and Ḥamilat their daughters, and the children of the said Ḥatibat and Ḥamilat, and for whomever produces a signed writ by the hand of Arwas or by his sisters Ḥatibat and Ḥamilat, daughters of Farwan the hipparch, only he may be buried in this tomb who has such a writ, only he may be justified in burying in this tomb. In the month of Nisan in the year thirty-six of Aretas, king of the Nabateans, who loves his people. Made by Aftah son of Abdobodat and Ḥuru son of Uḥayyu, sculptors."

manded only by a chiliarch and a centurion. Then, beginning in 27 C.E., a large number of strategoi, hipparchs, and other military administrative officeholders suddenly appeared at Egra—so many that it seems, at least, that most of the high-ranking Nabatean personnel were present at Egra during the second quarter of the first century C.E. Moreover, at a place in the vicinity of Egra, which the local Arabs named Kubur el-Gindi (Tombs of the Soldiers), numerous additional inscriptions were discovered that mention equites of the units named ala Flavia Dromedariorum and Getules, as well as a body named epitropeia, apparently composed of members of the Nabatean government; a man who served as a standard-bearer; a surveyor, and others. I concluded that the presence of a great part of the Nabatean army, assisted by mercenaries (who were sent by the Roman authorities to help the Nabateans) attest that the Nabatean kingdom faced a major emergency. I attempted to link this emergency with the evacuation of the Nabatean military camp of Oboda (sometime in the first half of the first century c.e.) and with the destruction and abandonment of Oboda about 50 c.e. I attributed these events to the Safaitic- and Thamudic-writing Arab tribes, whose inscriptions were found in the general area of Oboda. (Thousands of inscriptions of this kind cover the rocks of northern Arabia and southern Jordan.)[270] It is possible that at the beginning of the second quarter of the first century c.e. these tribes infiltrated the weakening Nabatean kingdom in order to pillage it. For about one generation the Nabateans vainly struggled to halt such infiltration, but in vain. The immediate result was a decline in monument making at Egra until it finally ceased in 75 c.e. and the destruction of the Nabatean caravan system in the Negev along the Petra–Gaza road.[271]

More recently, assistance in the matter of chronology came from the field of numismatics.[272] The silver content of Nabatean coins fluctuated markedly. From the beginning of the minting of silver from about 60 b.c.e. to 7 c.e., Nabatean silver kept pace with Roman silver, ranging from 96 to 87 percent silver content at the beginning to 72 to 62 percent in 7 c.e. In that same year silver content dropped to 54 to 41 percent and declined slowly until it reached the level of 20 percent silver in 50 c.e. It remained at this level until 72 c.e., when it rose to 42.5 percent. It stayed at this relatively high level until 78 c.e. but dropped again in 80 c.e. to the low level of 20 percent, from which it did not rise until toward the end of Nabatean minting in 100 c.e.

There is no more sensitive instrument for evaluating an economic and political situation than the state of the currency, whether in ancient or in modern times. The high level of silver in Nabatean currency in the early years may be explained as an attempt to keep pace with the value of Roman currency, so that the Nabateans were able to pay for the commodities acquired in India, eastern Africa, and southern Arabia, as well as for the services that the caravan trade involved.[273] Aelius Gallus's campaign against the Arabians in

11. The silver content of Nabatean coins. Drawing by Mrs. Anat Negev-Palti.

25 or 24 B.C.E. had little effect on the Nabatean economy, except for a 10 percent drop in the silver content of the currency. As already mentioned, it was in 7 C.E. that the silver content began to drop sharply, and I believe that Strabo's statement about the change in the fortunes of the Nabatean spice trade refers to this year.[274] As far as Nabatean chronology is concerned, the years 50 to 73 C.E., in which silver content remained at an inflation level of 20 percent, are of more interest: these were the years in which Oboda and other Nabatean sites in the Negev lay in ruins and in which Egra declined sharply. In an earlier work, I dated the change in Nabatean fortunes at Oboda to 80 C.E. when, possibly on the initiative of King Rabel, the Nabateans began to construct dams for purposes of irrigation.[275] This suggestion may be confirmed by the monetary situation. Rabel was a minor when he became king. On attaining maturity in the third year of his reign, Rabel may have begun to improve the state of the Nabatean economy by consolidating the currency. Inflation set in again in year 80 C.E., perhaps as a result of the immense investments that the construction of dams and farms involved. I believe that this threefold examination of the chronology of the Middle Nabatean period that is (1) the history of Oboda, (2) the history of Egra and (3) the history of Nabatean silver minting may now be taken as conclusive, and the dates as final.

28

Development of Nabatean Architecture and Urbanism

Nabatean material culture was different from that of the people who cultivated the land. This may be illustrated by the development of Nabatean pottery. At Oboda I dated the beginning of Nabatean pottery to 25 B.C.E. Peter Parr has dated similar pottery at Petra to about two generations earlier.[1] Whoever is right, Nabatean pottery making did not antedate the first century B.C.E. But, as we have already seen, Nabatean history began not later than the fourth century B.C.E., and as I proposed earlier it could well have begun in the seventh or the eighth century B.C.E. (p. 2). No pottery that may be identified as Nabatean was produced from the eighth to the first century B.C.E. Moreover, the only pottery found on sites that were later inhabited by the Nabateans was not made earlier than the late fourth to the early third century B.C.E.: this is the case at Petra,[2] Nessana,[3] Oboda,[4] and Elusa.[5] This phenomenon may be explained in only one way: the Nabateans, like other nomads, had no need for

29

pottery. That they were indeed nomads one may learn from the Hieronymus-Diodorus account cited earlier, and they were still nomads at about the middle of the second century B.C.E. In the early stages of their wars the Maccabees Judas and Jonathan met the Nabateans after a three-day march in the desert (1 Macc. 5:25–26). In 2 Maccabees, with all probability referring to the same people, we read: "The defeated nomads . . . went back to their tents" (12:11).[6] Since the Nabateans had little use for pottery and preferred the use of unbreakable waterskins and wooden bowls, the comparatively small amount of Hellenistic pottery found on Nabatean sites must have come by way of trade. What is astounding, however, is that the earliest-known pottery produced by the Nabateans in the first century B.C.E. is not of a primitive type, as would be expected of a people of little sophistication, and as is true of the pottery found on southern Arabian sites.[7] The earliest-known Nabatean pottery was the best of its time in the whole region of Palestine-Syria.[8] It was only in the later stages of Nabatean history that Nabatean pottery attained—or rather declined—to the standards of the pottery common to the whole region, of which the Nabateans formed a part.

I call this irregular course of development anomalous. Although it is a well-established archaeological fact, I have no good explanation for it, and as we shall see in the following pages, Nabatean architecture is no different. In fifty-five years of excavations on Nabatean sites no building remains of the Hellenistic period have come to light. The Horsfields' excavations at Petra were conducted mainly in city dumps, and it is from those that most of the Hellenistic pottery comes. The excavators at Nessana[9] identified a building they labeled "Hellenistic" at the eastern edge of the acropolis hill: "The earliest building on the site was the rectangular structure. . . . The south wall of this work was successively incorporated in the two later buildings on each of its sides surviving by virtue of the massiveness of its construction, and still stands as the highest feature of the hill. No foundations below, or earlier than those of the building, were found on the site, and it must be taken to be the first of any substantial character. The period of the building is established as Hellenistic by the pottery, found undisturbed in its foundation trenches and floor levels, and this evidence is further strengthened by the results of the excavations of a similar building at Abda." The Colt expedition published the plan of this building at Oboda[10] but mentioned no pottery. I had a chance to re-excavate this building in

30

1958–59, and the pottery found at the foundations was purely Middle Nabatean-early Roman, and was exactly the same as types found in the Nabatean potter's workshop. An examination of the pottery report of Nessana, compiled by J. T. C. Baly,[11] reveals where the mistake in this dating lies. For Baly, "Hellenistic" means "Before A.D. 106" and "Roman" means "A.D. 106–395."[12] From the Fort (i.e., the "Hellenistic Building") the Colt expedition published drawings and designations of three sherds only; two are "Megarian" bowls,[13] and the other is an unidentified piece of pottery, probably not glazed.[14] The rest of the pottery, which comes from the outside the Fort–North Church complex, is totally mixed, from Hellenistic to late Byzantine. Taking into account what we now know of the history of the Nabatean Negev, the Hellenistic pottery of Nessana pertains to the preconstruction period, and the Fort itself is not Hellenistic but Middle Nabatean.

Only recently did R. Cohen make a new attempt to identify a building of the Hellenistic period underneath the large caravansery at so-called Moa in the Arabah.[15] The pottery found in the lowest level of occupation is indeed Hellenistic (of the third and second centuries B.C.E.), but according to the excavator[16] the building has only one floor, which is connected with the massive walls of the caravansery, and he finds it difficult to assign it to either the Middle Nabatean or the Hellenistic period. There is no escape from the conclusion that the early pottery of Moa pertains to the preconstruction period, whereas that of the Middle Nabatean period pertains to the caravansery.

No other site reveals the complexity of the history of Nabatean architecture as does Petra, the capital of the Nabatean kingdom. The only worthwhile attempt to study the history of construction at Petra was made by Peter J. Parr.[17] He concludes: "Three main stages may be discerned in the architectural development of this part of Petra: an initial stage of small buildings of unpretentious design and construction (Phases I–VIII).[18] A second stage, of monumental structures belonging to an ambitious civic plan (Phase IX),[19] and a third stage, when the paved street was constructed, perhaps superseding an earlier thoroughfare (Phase XIII)."[20] Whatever the case, no buildings of the Hellenistic period proper were discovered at Petra.

It is thus obvious that, despite the fact that Nabatean sites were occupied in the Hellenistic period, no building remains of this period have been found. My theory is that in this early stage of their history the Nabateans lived in tent encampments. The anomaly of the history of Nabatean architecture becomes even more obvious when the Middle Nabatean period is reviewed.

That the Nabateans were both experienced sculptors and great builders does not need much substantiation. We have no information about the artisans who sculpted the almost 1,000 funerary monuments at Petra, but we are well informed about the identity of the makers of the tombs at Egra. Many of the monuments made for the upper class of residents of Egra were signed by one or two artists who belonged to families of sculptors or artists—amana, as they named themselves in the detailed inscriptions engraved on the facades of almost half of the monuments.[21] Thus are mentioned Wahab-ʾallahi son of ʿAbd-ʿabdat; Ḥalf-ʾallahi, the sculptor; and Ruma and ʿAbd-ʿabdat, sculptors. Architects, masons, and plasterers who were engaged in the construction of the Nabatean temple at Iram signed their names in the same way.[22] Nabatean architects and artists are also mentioned in Nabatean inscriptions in the Hauran.[23] Also, a Nabatean plasterer is mentioned at Petra.[24] Not only were the artisans Nabatean but also the artistic elements they produced, such as the capital, or the specific combination of the different artistic elements, were Nabatean.

I believe that what has confused many scholars are Strabo's statements about the Nabateans. Strabo was in Egypt in 25 and 24 B.C.E., accompanying Aelius Gallus in his campaign to the frontiers of Ethiopia (see *Geog.* II.5.12); in fact, he was still in Egypt in 20 B.C.E. (see XIV.1.14), where he probably spent several years. Strabo never went east, however, and in his account of the Nabateans he had to rely on the words of "Athenodorus, a philosopher and companion of mine" (XVI.4.21). Alongside the sound facts about the geography of Petra we also find a statement like: "They have the same regard for the dead as for dung . . . and therefore they bury even their kings beside dung-heaps" (XVI.2.26). We shall return to this statement in Chapter III. The other statement, possibly also relying on Athenodorus's evidence, is: "Their homes, through the use of stone, are costly, but on account of peace, their cities are not walled" (XVI.4.26). Should we treat Petra as a city as meaning a habitable place extending over an area of more than 250 acres, enclosed by rocks? Strabo writes: "The metropolis of the Nabateans is Petra, as it is called, for it lies on a site which is otherwise smooth and level,

32

12. Egra. A Nabatean tomb decorated by two rows of crenellations. The door is surmounted by an arch, an eagle, and three urns. Note the inscription above.

but it is fortified all around by a rock, the outside parts of the site being precipitous and sheer, and the inside parts having springs in abundance, both for domestic purposes and watering gardens" (XVI.4.26).

A journalist writing about Petra states: "They had to contend with the problem that, at the height of its prosperity, the city area itself probably housed between 18,000 and 20,000 persons. With the various suburbs such as Wadi Siyagh, el-Sabrah, el-Barid, el-Madras, etc., the total would have been as great as 30,000."[25] If we continued this line of thought, then the total number of houses at Petra would have ranged between 360 and 600, counting 50 persons to a house. So many houses should have left a considerable number of ruins that would still be available for examination, considering that the local Bedouins would have had little use for building materials. But no such ruins are present either at Petra or at any of the "suburbs" mentioned in the above quotation. Browning writes: "It is amazing that a race so expert in rock excavation should have been so unskilled in building. Nabatean buildings erected before the annexation are astonishingly poorly built. . . . The Nabatean city, before the annexation, would have had the look of any prosperous Arab town up to a decade ago before the modern building techniques ruined an urban tradition which lasted for thousands of years. . . . Houses would have been of a single storey, huddled together along narrow, twisting gravel-trod lanes, each built round its own semi-porticoed courtyard. Roofs would have been flat and windows

13. Petra. A Nabatean house excavated in the rock.

34

regular and small. The temple and markets provided the only large-scale spaces in this human ant-hill but harsh straight lines would have been relieved by the use of bright colours on the plastered walls and cornices. Only those buildings of stately proportions would have had any pretensions to architecture and even these would have had an Arab simplicity and strength wholly different from the Western tradition."[26]

I have quoted the above passages because of the fact that such views are also privately expressed by scholars concerned with Petra and Nabateans. In fact, the only private houses so far investigated at Petra are those surveyed by the Horsfields and by Murray and Ellis. The Horsfields published photographs of several man-made excavated caves, one of which is the famous "Painted House" at Siq el-Barid.[27] Murray and Ellis excavated two caves along what they believed to be a street, running above the southern bank of Wadi Olleqa.[28] The North Cave was excavated mostly from rock, but there is a segment of a wall of good-quality masonry at its entrance.[29] The

14. Petra. The theater in the midst of the necropolis. (Elia Photo-Service, Jerusalem).

35

15. Petra. The cavea of the theater. Note the destroyed tombs in the background. (Elia Photo-Service, Jerusalem).

South Cave was used for burial. In this tomb too there is good-quality masonry. According to the excavators, this tomb complex was excavated "at least as early as the first century B.C. or earlier."[30] These in fact are all the "houses" that have been excavated at Petra.

So, this is how the metropolis of the Nabateans supposedly looked at the peak of its prosperity. I am not willing to accept it. I claim that in the last quarter of the first century B.C.E. and in the first century C.E. Petra was not mostly a city of the living. It was a huge religious center, with several temples,[31] as well as a festival theater, a nymphaeum, a bathhouse, a sacred way, a monumental gate, and several other public buildings. The other component of this large religious center was the city of the dead. Whereas the temples and other public buildings occupied the central valley, the necropolis extended over the eastern rock wall, where the "Royal Tombs" were situated, and encompassed the wadis emptying into the valley. This was Petra as I see it. But questions remain: Where did the citizens of Petra live? And where did the hundreds of gravediggers, monument sculptors, temple attendants, and other functionaries supervis-

36

16. Petra. The Khaznet Faraʿun, "Treasury of Pharaoh." Possibly the tomb of Aretas IV, this is probably the only monument at Petra made by Alexandrian artists.

17. Petra. Partial view of the necropolis. Notice the one- and two-row crenellated tombs.

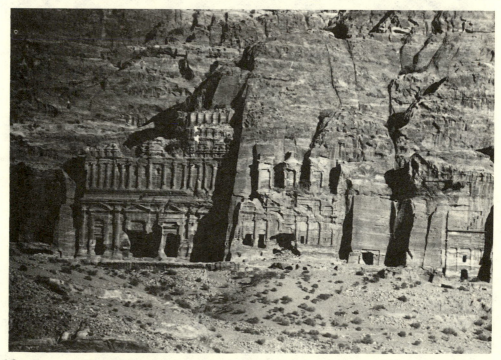

18. Petra. The "Royal Tombs." The "Palace Tomb" is on the left, and the Corinthian Tomb is on the right.

38

19. Petra. The "Palace Tomb." The side entrances probably led to triclinia.

20. Petra. Qasr Bint Faraʿun. In the foreground are steps of the theatron, where festive meals were served. (Elia Photo-Service, Jerusalem).

ing this immense religious center live? I believe that most of them lived in tents as they did in the Early Nabatean period. Thus, archaeologists must look on the other side of the Arabah for the remains of such encampments.

Petra was not the only religious center in the Nabatean realm. At the south is the little-investigated center of Egra, about which we have knowledge only of the necropolis and a rock-cut sanctuary.[32] Then there is the religious center of Iram, with its temple, military installation, and necropolis.[33] Northeast of Petra is Khirbet et-Tannur, of which only the temple has been investigated.[34] We know very little about Nabatean Moab, but in Auranitis we find the religious center of Seeia with its three temples and a necropolis.[35] This is what the Nabatean kingdom to the east of the Arabah and the Jordan looked like in the Middle Nabatean period.

In the Negev, only Oboda of the Middle Nabatean period has been extensively investigated. During this period Oboda consisted of a temple, a military camp, and enclosures for camel breeding. The temple and the camp, built long before the Roman Empire's annexation of the Nabatean kingdom, were constructed by expert masons and, as we have seen, by architects and masons, all of whom were Nabateans. From the beginning of my work in the Negev I looked hard for dwellings of the Middle Nabatean period. Three years of extensive excavations at Oboda produced none. It was not until 1977 that remains of a large building were excavated less than fifty meters to the northeast of the Nabatean military camp. It consisted of a large court adjacent to which were small rooms, or cubicles.[36] The pottery on the earthen floors was of the Middle Nabatean period, conforming to the pottery found in the towers of the camp. The building was made of fieldstones set in mud mortar. There was nothing in the finds that would indicate the function of this building, but its proximity to the military camp and the size of the cubicles suggest that services were rendered in it of a kind needed by a large number of males who were perhaps living at Oboda without their families. If this supposition is correct, then this too was a public building, not a private dwelling.

By the early 1960s I had already conceived the idea that Middle Nabatean Oboda was essentially a public project where the people lived in tents. Thus, when I was given the chance to excavate at Mampsis, I planned to search for private buildings of the Middle Nabatean period. That this site was indeed occupied during the first half of the first century C.E. I learned from pottery found in the

40

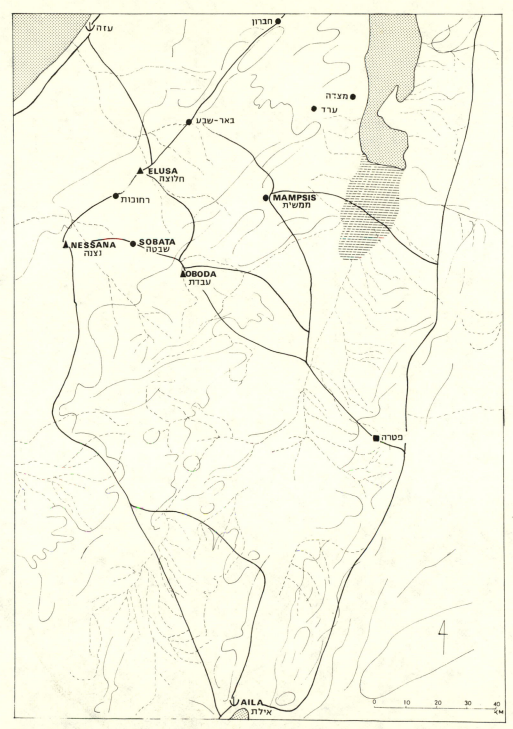

21. Nabatean caravan routes in the Negev. Drawing by Mrs. Anat Negev-Palti.

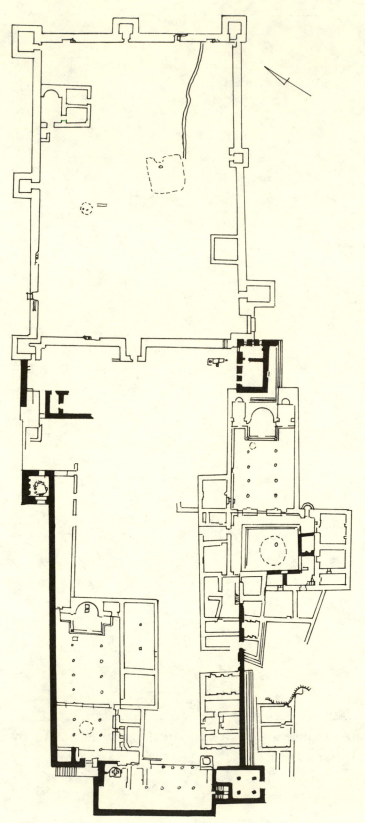

22. Oboda. Plan of the acropolis. Buildings of the Middle and Late
Nabatean periods are indicated by solid lines. (A. Engel).

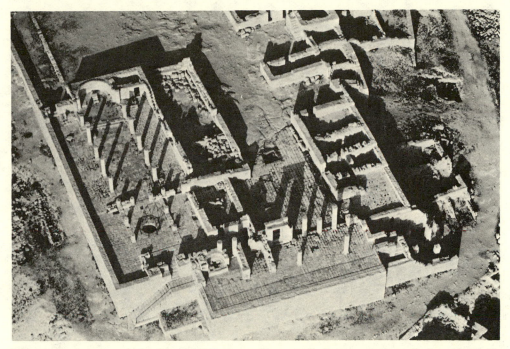

23. Oboda. Aerial view of the podium of the temple of the Middle Nabatean period showing the superimposed Christian church. Photograph by Dr. R. Cleave.

local Nabatean necropolis.[37] The first structure of the Middle Nabatean period that my team investigated in the city was a caravansery (Building VIII),[38] which was obviously a public institution. A fortress (Building XIV) built at the southeastern part of the hill, of which only one half was preserved, also belongs to the Middle Nabatean period. A typical watchtower, incorporated in the Late Nabatean market building (Building IV), also dates from this period. These are all public structures. The only complex of buildings that seem to be private ones are Buildings XIX and Va, located in the northeastern part of the town. Their date is determined by the fact that they underlie Late Nabatean Building VII, a public reservoir, and Building V, a bathhouse, as well as by the pottery, which is Middle Nabatean. Building XIX is a courthouse type of building and is composed of four oblong storerooms of the type found at Masada.[39] The character of the storerooms leads one to suspect that this too was a public storehouse and that the whole building was a caravansery. Because of the overlying bathhouse, it was impossible

43

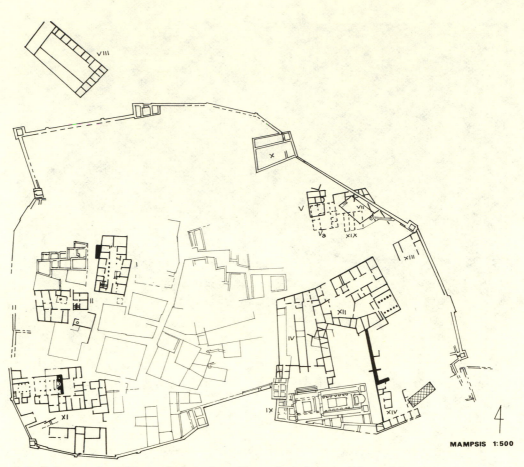

MAMPSIS 1:500

24. Mampsis. Plan of the site. Drawing by A. Urweider.

to excavate all of Building Va, so that the nature of the older structure could not be determined. I believe that the fact that four of the five buildings of the Middle Nabatean period partly investigated at Mampsis are definitely public in nature is not the result of chance.

Mampsis of the Late Nabatean period leaves no doubt that it was a place at which the Nabateans—descendants of tent dwellers only one or two generations earlier—built a city in the proper sense of the word.

As we saw in Chapter I, the Nabatean settlement in the Negev ended in a disaster about 50 C.E. The military camp at Oboda was deserted and the temple was destroyed by fire probably long before that date. Other road stations along the route leading from the Arabah to Oboda and from there to Elusa and Mampsis suffered the same fate.[40] Apparently, Oboda was a completely deserted city until

44

25. Mampsis. Aerial view looking northeast. Photograph by Dr. R. Cleave.

about 80 C.E.,[41] when former Nabatean caravan traders embarked on a new enterprise, heretofore completely alien to them, that decided the fortunes of this region and the Nabateans for many generations: agriculture.

Indeed, there are statements in Strabo that reflect the Middle Nabatean period that still have to be explained. In one passage Strabo writes: "The inside parts [of Petra have] springs in abundance, both for domestic purposes and for watering gardens" (XVI.4.21). These "domestic purposes" could have been the water supply of the temples, the bathhouse, the theater, and the nymphaeum; the gardens were perhaps of a kind referred to in the large Nabatean inscription engraved on the facade of the monument known as Qasr el-Turkman at Petra (*CIS* II, 350). The second line of this inscription speaks of gardens and water installations pertaining to this tomb.[42] Another statement of Strabo requiring explanation is: "Most of the country is well supplied with fruits, except the olive; they use sesame-oil instead" (XVI.4.21). This could well refer either to southern Moab or to southern Auranitis, both of which were occupied by the Na-

45

bateans in this period; in these territories the Nabateans formed only part of the population, and agriculture could have been practiced by the autochthonic residents. The chronology of agriculture in the Negev itself has not yet been worked out.[43]

It is quite certain, however, that in the central Negev the development of Nabatean agriculture began in the last two decades of the first century C.E. It is also certain that horse breeding was one of the major enterprises of the Nabatean cities of the Negev. So far the evidence for this comes mainly from Mampsis, but stables of the Mampsis type have also been discovered at Oboda and Sobata.

The impact of the new way of life on the Nabateans must have been tremendous. At least that part of the Nabatean population that turned to agriculture left their tents for good. Those who have been educated in the West, or in the Western tradition, will certainly consider that this change meant better living conditions—but was that the case? The Acropolis of classical Athens, the Forum of Rome, and the public quarters of other classical, Hellenistic, or Roman cities notwithstanding, life in a city or a village in the ancient world offered its inhabitants little comfort. Streets were narrow; houses were crowded; and sanitary conditions were far from satisfactory.

26. Oboda. Libation altar with a Nabatean inscription of 88/89 C.E. commemorating the beginning of Nabatean agriculture. (A. Volk).

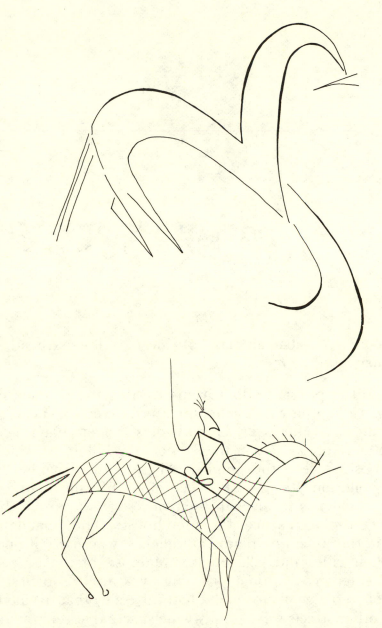

27. Oboda. Drawing of a mare and a colt on wet plaster, 293/94 C.E. Copied by T. Rabani.

By comparison, life in a tent encampment was rather comfortable. Separate tents were allotted to men, to women and children, and to visitors; others were used for storage. Horses and camels were located within watching distance of the tents but were far enough away

28. Oboda. A Nabatean clay figurine of a horse's head, found in the Nabatean dump.

to prevent unpleasant odors from affecting the people. Sheep and goats were kept in rock shelters, natural caves, or enclosures made of brushwood. Moreover, because of seasonal changes in the climate, tents were located at the lee side of a hill in the winter and on the opposite side in the summer. These annual changes also minimized pollution. It must have been quite difficult for the freedom-loving Nabateans to give up their ancestral ways of living and to exchange the open spaces for stone houses. The inhabitants of Palestine in the Byzantine period are generally accused of poorly planning their cities and villages. But Mampsis of the Late Nabatean period antedates this poor planning by several centuries. The only street of some length formed a natural gulley that drained the city; all the other streets were simply wide spaces that separated dwelling blocks, thus providing for maximum privacy. The public structures—the caravansery (Building VIII), the reservoir (Building VII), and the bathhouse (Building V)—were completely separated from the rest of the town. Another bathhouse, which has not been excavated, is situated in a separate block in the southern part of the town, between Street 1 and Street 12, not far from the escarpment of the wadi.

48

The size of the dwellings is striking. The smallest private house excavated at Mampsis (Building XI) extends over an area of 700 square meters; the largest (Building XII) extends over an area of 2,000 square meters; a semipublic house, identified as a palace (Building I), occupies an area of 1,000 square meters; and a watchtower (Building II) extends over the typical area of 100 square meters, though its court, suite of adjoining rooms, and storerooms increase the extent of the complex to about 800 square meters. All these houses were two and sometimes three stories high, which added to the usable living space. There is little doubt that each of these houses was made to accommodate one family. Of course, wealth had much to do with the construction of dwellings of these dimensions. Since their size is unique in Palestine, however, an additional explanation has to be sought as well. The tradition of amplitude in the Negev continued into the Byzantine period, at which time at Oboda in a stone-built house the living and working space was enlarged by the addition of a man-made cave, which was joined to the house by a corridor. I believe that the unusual size of the Nabatean house was intended to compensate the Nabateans for the loss of freedom and the spaciousness of the life in tent encampments. It is, of course, difficult to prove this theory, but wealth does not seem to have been the only reason for the size of the Nabatean buildings at Mampsis. The Nabateans were not the only rich people in Palestine, though their dwellings are far larger than those of the richest Jerusalemites of the Second Temple period.

Nabatean houses at Mampsis and, as far as we have been able to ascertain, at other sites in the Negev, stand out also by virtue of the materials from which they were built. The Negev lacks trees of any size suitable for construction and roofing. Although the plains are rich in brickmaking materials, the Nabateans never resorted to bricks except in making the hypocausts in bathhouses. The only other material available to them was stone. On the acropolis hill of Oboda we had a chance to learn the method by which Nabateans were able to cut large blocks of stone. In order to level off a site for the construction of the temple, holes 10 to 15 centimeters wide were driven into the living rock. Logs of dry wood were placed in these holes; then water was poured into them. When the dry logs expanded, a fissure formed along the row of holes. The rest of the work was done with iron tools. In order to provide the large blocks of stone necessary for the construction of the walls of the temple, a quarry was opened about one kilometer downslope from the site of construction, at the northern part of the hill. At this place there are natural layers of hard rock 80 to 100 centimeters high, which are equivalent to the height of the courses of the temple walls. Thus, it was comparatively easy for workmen to detach large blocks of stone from these natural layers. One of these blocks, on which a rectangle had been marked by a sharp tool as guidelines for the stonecutter, was left in the quarry because of a fissure in one of its corners. We also discovered the narrow upsloping path by which the one- to two-ton building blocks were transported to the building site. At Mampsis, too, we discovered building blocks 2 to 4 meters long at the base of the tower. The quarry at Mampsis is located on the other side of the wadi, southwest of the city, which also necessitated upslope transportation of the heavy building blocks.

The only difference between the Middle and Late Nabatean periods is that in the latter period smaller building stones were used in construction. Furthermore, the regions of Oboda and Mampsis offer a great variety of stone for construction, from the softest and lightest chalk to the hardest and heaviest dolomite, which is almost like marble in quality. As a rule, the Nabateans preferred the harder and more durable stone, which meant more and costlier work. At Elusa, which is closer to sea level than the other cities, and at which only chalk is exposed, the Nabateans took the trouble of traveling to the mountainous region southwest of the city, a distance of five to six kilometers, in order to obtain stone to their liking. The hardest stone was always used for the construction of a building's lower story, whereas the upper stories were built of lighter stone, though never of chalk. Chalk was not used for construction of walls in the Negev before the Byzantine period. The lack of timber was acutely felt in connection with roofing, but this problem was easily solved. In the Middle Nabatean period, the gates leading to the temple at Oboda were partly roofed by arches with slabs of stone above them. It was the quality of these slabs that determined the method of roofing in the central Negev. In numerous places the mountains of the central Negev are covered by a thin layer (5–10 cm) of hard stone, which is easily peeled off and is easy to break down to workable sizes. Sometimes these layers consist of softer, less durable stone. The drawback in using this stone is that it tends to break if the slabs are cut too long. This factor determined the spacing of the arches. A medium-hard stone was used to make the segments of the arches.

50

The arch either sprang directly out of the wall or was supported by pilasters attached to the wall. In some cases, the arch was a direct continuation of the pilaster; in other cases, the pilaster and the arch were separated by a cap, which sometimes had a simple decoration. The arches were placed from 80 to 100 centimeters from each other. The triangular space that was formed between the side walls, the roof, and the arch was filled with quarry waste and mud mortar. The arches, which had a maximum diameter of 6 meters, had no keystones, but the center stone was sometimes embellished by sculpture. Though the width of the room was thus limited to 6 meters, there was no limit to its length. The Nabateans employed the same method of roofing in the cities and villages in Auranitis,[44] but owing to the use of harder basalt, the spacing of the arches was not as close as in the central Negev, and some of the narrower spaces that in the Negev required arches were roofed by corbels and a longer slab of stone in Auranitis.[45] There is no way of determining where Nabatean construction developed first—in the Negev, in Auranitis, or in both regions simultaneously.

More important was the matter of insulation. The differences in temperature between day and night and summer and winter are extremely large. Thus, at Oboda the mean temperature is 18.2° C; the mean annual maximum temperature is 46.4° (1° less than at Eilat!); the mean minimum temperature of the coldest month is 10.2°.[46] Under such conditions the builders of the Nabatean dwellings in the Negev were expected to provide for protection from the heat in the summer and, with few combustibles for heating, also from the severe cold of the winter. These problems were tackled by constructing houses of maximal insulation. The exterior walls were made of three layers. The outer shell consisted of well-polished ashlars that were laid dry, and the accurate fitting of the stones prevented as far as possible the penetration of moisture. The inner shell, facing the interior of the room, was made of coarsly cut blocks of stone, with a filling of small stones and mud in the joints. Between the two layers was a filling of quarry waste and mud that provided additional insulation.

The interior of the room was then covered with several layers of plaster, beginning with mud plaster to fill the joints and cover the coarse face of the stone, and ending with layers of finer plaster. The walls were then whitewashed with fine lime plaster to form a base for frescoes. Interior walls of courts were sometimes treated in the

51

same way as the interior walls of living rooms. Insulation was also achieved by taking the size and number of windows into consideration. These were narrow on the outside, somewhat wider on the inside, and were placed at the tops of the walls, just below the ceiling.[47] These windows, which resemble archers' slots, supplied air and light while preventing as far as possible the penetration of drafts and dust. The way doors were made and placed also played an important role in insulation. Doors were always made of wood set in wooden frames. Doors of living rooms always opened on the south or west. Thus, in the winter, when the sun is low, the rooms were flooded by the sun through the open doors. In the summer, when the sun is high, the open doors let in the pleasant breeze coming from the sea most of the day while avoiding the penetration of the sun's scorching rays. In some buildings at Oboda, Mampsis, and Sobata everything except for the wooden doors was preserved intact and still serve as excellent shelters in both winter and summer. Other principal features of Nabatean domestic architecture will be described in reference to the various buildings excavated at Mampsis.

First let us consider Building II (a tower). That towers of this kind were built at Mampsis in the Middle Nabatean period has already been mentioned (p. 50). And we are not certain that Building II was built in the Late Nabatean period. The building blocks of the lower two courses of its eastern face[48] are 2 to 4 meters long, and these seem to be uncharacteristic of the Late Nabatean period. Nothing has been found on the floors earlier than the Byzantine period, which is the latest period of its use. However, since the large size of the building blocks is typical of the Middle Nabatean period, its exact dating remains uncertain. Its plan shows three rooms and a staircase-tower. Although the staircase-tower was not a Nabatean invention, it became a customary feature of Nabatean sacred architecture in the Middle Nabatean period and came into use in domestic architecture in the Late Nabatean period.[49] The convenient but costly means of access to the second and third stories of Building II raised it to an approximate height of about 12 meters. From it one could observe the life-giving dams in the wadi to the southwest of the town, the plain to the north and west, and the road coming up from the Arabah to the east. The court to the west of the tower is paved by polished slabs of stone, a feature common to all living rooms and inner courts of buildings. This floor also served as a roof of a cistern excavated in the rock underneath it. The cistern has a

52

29. Mampsis. Building II: the tower and its court. (R. Brody).

barrel-vaulted roof made of ashlars. South of the court is a suite of three rooms consisting of a large one in the middle and narrow, oblong rooms on each side, which probably served as official guest-houses. West of the court are two oblong storerooms with arched roofs. These rooms, and the storerooms of Middle Nabatean Building XIX (see p. 43), are the only suites of this type that have been discovered in the Nabatean Negev. North of the court is a kitchen with two ovens and a stone-built workbench. Several steps at the northeast corner of the court lead up to a small platform, which was probably used to unload standing donkeys or kneeling camels. Finally, a channel was built against the east wall of the suite; this channel carried water that was poured into it to an underground channel, which in turn emptied into the cistern. It was probably installed to prevent water carriers, enlisted from among the seminomads who lived in the vicinity of the town, from entering the court. At Mampsis, similar channels serving the same purposes were also observed in buildings of the late Roman and Byzantine periods.

Towers became a standard feature of Nabatean military architecture from the Middle Nabatean period at least through the end of the third century C.E. The existence of towers at Mampsis has been noted by Woolley and Lawrence, who distinguished between the "Fort" (our Building II) and a series of "blockhouses," by which the western and eastern dams ("barrages," in their terminology) were protected: "The strategic importance of Kurnub is emphasized by the system of blockhouses that secure its command over the ravine road. . . . These six towers, dependent upon the main fort, occupying the posts of vantage that best command the south road and the gorge, give the place a character quite different from that of any other of these southern cities."[50] Because of the lack of city walls, except for the rather flimsy wall built at Mampsis by the end of the third century C.E., the tower constituted these cities' only means of defense. This was certainly the case of Elusa, the defense of which was based on lines of towers. In 1973[51] my team and I investigated one of these, rising above the southern bank of Nahal Atadim. In the course of our survey we also noted a line of towers along the spine of the city, facing Nahal Besor to the south. One of these towers was partly excavated in 1980.[52] In its plan and in the solidity of its walls it resembles Building II at Mampsis. We have as yet no date for these towers, but they quite certainly were still in use in the late Roman period. At Oboda a large tower was erected in 293/94 C.E.[53] at the southern end of the small town of the late Roman period. It is noteworthy that the architect who built it was Wailos (Wailu in Nabatean) from Petra. This is the latest-dated typical staircase-tower constructed in the Negev. No towers of this type have been discovered in the other three towns of the central Negev.

Building I, the "Palace," is a completely different type of building. Despite its spaciousness, it is very compactly built. Because of the lack of a city wall in the Late Nabatean period, it was made as a self-contained fortress. It has only one entrance, which is on the south. It opened on a paved vestibulum (6.0 × 2.80 m), flanked by a small guardroom on the west. From the vestibulum one entered a paved court (13.0 × 8.50 m). There were several units opening on the court, each with a different function: on the east, a reception

54

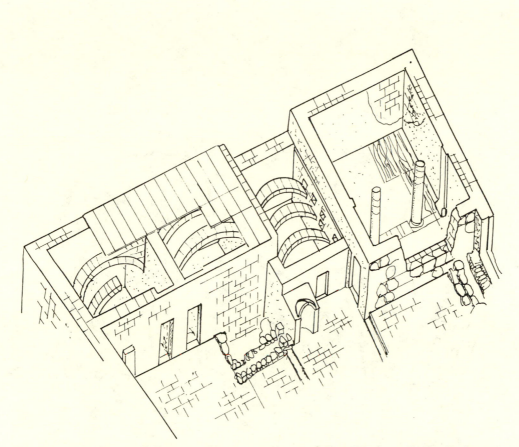

30. Mampsis. Building I: the east wing of the "Palace." (B. Brimer).

hall, a library and archive, a kitchen and bakery, servants' rooms, and two deep storerooms; on the west, large storerooms; and on the north, living rooms. One-third of the reception hall was covered, its roof resting on two attached pilasters and on two freestanding columns. The walls were plastered and whitewashed. The floor of the whole room was made of wood, its supporting beams resting on stone ledges built at the lower part of the side walls and on a cross-wall in the middle of the large open space. The wooden threshold was found intact, and some of the floor planks were also found in the debris. In the wall near the entrance is a large niche for holding a torch. The library, which adjoins the reception hall, occupies a lower level and was entered by several steps.[54] The roof of the small, unpaved room was made of three arches, all of which have been preserved intact. The south wall, between the arches, contains built-in cupboards with stone shelves. I believe that this room served as a

55

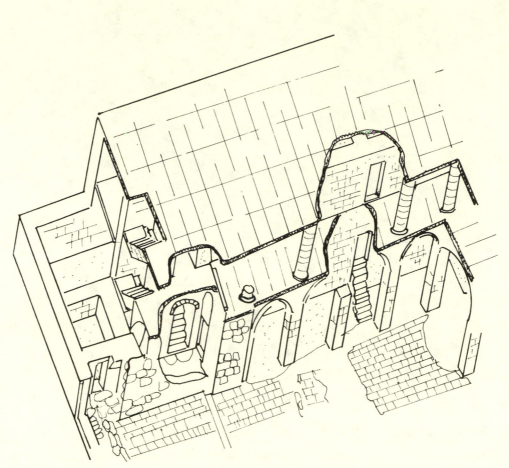

31. Mampsis. Building I: the west wing of the "Palace." (B. Brimer).

library, or more likely as an archive, perhaps for the preservation of documents relating to horse breeding, the main source of income at Mampsis in the Late Nabatean period.

Next to the entrance to the library stands a curious installation: a semicircular structure, opening on the west, covered by a semi-dome, and made of one stone. On discovering it, we tended to identify it as a house shrine, but when another installation, which presumably served the same purpose, but opening on the north, was discovered in Building XI, it seemed to us that this niche once contained a large earthenware jar for keeping cooled water.

The two identical rooms to the north of the library were identified as servants' quarters on account of the lack of pavement, in contrast to all the other living rooms, which were stone-paved. The arches of all of the rooms in the east wing are supported by both

56

the north and the south walls, as statics would require. However, in the northernmost of these two rooms two systems of roofing arches were observed. One consisted of running in an east–west direction; the other consisted of arches springing out of the north and south walls. Since this phenomenon could hardly have been a mistake on the part of the architect, it was taken as an indication of the presence of an earlier phase in the history of the building, to which the set of the north–south arches belonged. Indeed, when the earthern floor of the room was excavated, a living level of the Middle Nabatean period was encountered. It contained typical Nabatean painted pottery and terra sigillata of the first century C.E. This date was corroborated by the discovery of two silver coins, of Aretas IV and Malichus II (40–70 C.E.) It is not certain whether these two rooms are connected with this earlier living phase or whether they indicate that a change of planning occurred at the beginning of the Late Nabatean period. In front of these two rooms are the remains of a large cooking and baking oven.

The last installation in the east wing consists of two curious small rooms with very high entrances. Each of these rooms was roofed over by a single arch. The lower part of both rooms is deeply cut in the rock. The only way to gain entrance to this part of these rooms is by means of wooden steps or ladders. These rooms probably served as storerooms for dried meat, salted fish, milk products, dried vegetables and fruits, and wine.

On the opposite, west side of the court there are two large storerooms and one small one. The two large rooms are entered by steep flights of steps. In their construction the Nabatean architect manifested one of his qualities—not to perform unnecessary work. Since these rooms were made to house products stored in jars and baskets, the floor, consisting of the natural rock, was never leveled off, and there is a difference in height of about 1 meter from one end of the room to the other. The small room is a nicely constructed chamber with a floor of beaten earth, and was possibly built as a storage room for valuables.

The north wing of Building I was constructed of unusually good masonry. Entrance to this wing is gained by a wide and deep vestibulum, roofed by four arches. The vestibulum was treated as a room interior and was plastered. At its west side is a rather small unpaved room which does not communicate with the living rooms and may have been the lodgings of personal attendants. On the opposite side, east of the vestibulum, is another small room, and attached to its south wall is a stone-built channel that empties on the street through an opening in the wall. This may have been a washroom. The living quarters consist of three rooms. One was a bedroom, as may be inferred from the three built-in cupboards in one of its walls. The openings were lined by ashlars, with typically decorated Nabatean doorpost capitals and bases. Some of the segments of the roofing arches were decorated by the typically Nabatean oblique stone dressing. The walls, except for the parts made of ashlars, were plastered and whitewashed.

In the southwest corner of the court is a staircase-tower that has been preserved intact except for the barrel vault by which its vestibulum was covered. The staircase-tower is connected with a device in the court that has not been found anywhere else. It consists of an L-shaped row of pillars, the first and last of which were attached to the walls of the court. The pillars supported six arches; two segments of the first pillars in the row were preserved in situ. The arches carried a wooden balcony, the planks of which were supported both by a groove in the east wall of the west wing and by the arches. Access to this suspended balcony was given by a gangway situated at the top of the vaulted vestibulum of the staircase-tower, at which the third flight of steps of the staircase-tower ended. The doors of three rooms of the west wing and of several other rooms of the north wing opened on this balcony, thus providing privacy for the persons residing in them. But this is not all. In the staircase-tower a fourth flight of steps leads either to a roof of the first floor or to an additional second floor. More evidence for the existence of another suspended balcony leading to this higher level was discovered in the course of the excavations of the court. A large number of column drums and matching bases and capitals were discovered between the L-shaped pillars and the wall. These column drums must have belonged to the second, upper suspended balcony. In reading the description of Building I at Mampsis, in the construction of which very little use of imagination was made, one should remember what has been said of Nabatean Petra before its annexation by the Roman Empire: "It is amazing that a race so expert in rock excavation should have been so unskilled in building."[55]

Except for the pottery, the coins, and the typically Nabatean stonework, little has been found to date this building. The finds on the floors were of the Byzanine period, during which it was still in

58

use. Unlike the other buildings at Mampsis, in which the water supply was always located in the inner court or in one of the rooms, the two cisterns of Building I were excavated in the small square in front of it. One of these was cleared; it had a capacity of about 200 cubic meters.

The third structure that has been fully excavated is Building XI, situated south of Buildings I and II, at the southwestern corner of the city. Building XI, the smallest private dwelling excavated at Mampsis, extends over an area of 700 square meters. The west half of the building was destroyed when a small church, the West Church, was built above it, though some of the rooms originally belonging to the earlier building were incorporated in the church complex. Building XI is entered through a rather large room at its northeast corner, which was probably the original entrance. On the north, one opening leads to a living room; another, on the west side, leads to a small rectangular court, almost half of which is now occupied by the church. An entrance to another living room is on the west wall of the court. In the court there is a small cistern, preserved intact. In the east wall of the court is an entrance to a staircase-tower of a type different from that of Buildings I and II. Whereas those have a square pier in their center, that of Building XI is rectangular. The

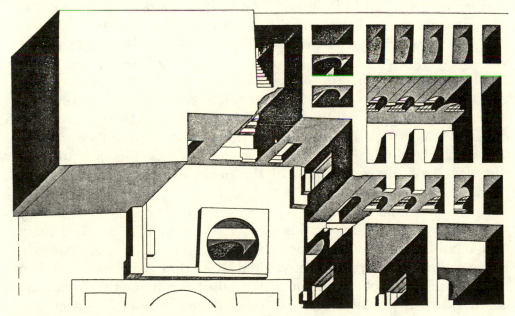

32. Mampsis. Building XI: reconstruction. (R. Livneh).

upper floor was gained by one long flight consisting of nine steps and by a short one consisting of two steps. Each of the steps also formed a building block of the central pier, which added to its stability. An additional long flight of steps, little of which remains, led to the upper story. The pier was made of ashlars, some of which are rather large, as required by the structure. In keeping with the fashion of the Late Nabatean period, during which small blocks of stone were preferred for reasons of economy, the masons divided them by false joints to create an appearance of a structure made of small stones. This was done only where these joints were illuminated by light and accordingly were seen by people entering the staircase-tower. Adjoining the staircase-tower is a small room, and on the south a device for keeping cool water is built into the wall, as in Building I.

A door on the south side of the court leads into the most important part of the house: the stable. The identification of this unusually well planned and well built part of the house is based on a comparison with similar structures in Nabatean Auranitis, but those in Auranitis were made of harder basalt, and, therefore, are less refined in form.[56] A single entrance leads into a basilican structure. It consists of a hall surmounted by four arches and of two narrow aisles. Each aisle is formed by a wall pierced by an arcuated door and by four arched "windows." The horses stood in the aisles, and the windows formed the troughs. Each trough was hollowed out of two stones, which also formed the heavy windowsills. Tethering devices were located at the sides of the supports of the arches of the windows. On the outside of the windows, facing the larger hall in which the fodder was kept, are arrangements for affixing grills; these were installed to prevent the horses from munching the fodder, which could damage their health. All the doors and windows were made of fine ashlars. On the top edges of the troughs one may still feel the effects of the smoothness of the necks of the animals that fed there.

The continuation of the court westward, now a narrow passage at a corner of the church, leads into a curious small room. It consists of a small forecourt that is open to the sky and of an inner chamber. Half of this chamber is barrel-vaulted; the other half has no roof. A tall rectangular niche is in the west wall of the hypaethral half. We could find no practical explanation for this chamber; it seems to have been a house shrine in a city in which there apparently was no

33. Building XI: the stable, looking west. (R. Brody).

monumental temple. An image of the deity was probably placed in the niche, and libations were poured and incense was burned on the flat roof of the vaulted chamber. This brings to mind Strabo's statement: "They worship the sun, building an altar on the top of the house, and pouring libations on it daily and burning frankincense" (XVI.4.26).

The three buildings described above are all situated in the western half of the town. Building XII is located in the eastern half. It extends over an area of approximately 2,000 square meters, and was a one-family unit. It was entered by a spacious vestibulum on the north. There are two small chambers to the right of the entrance: a guardroom and what may have been an office. A beautifully made arcuated entranceway leads into the interior of this large mansion where there is a large, irregularly shaped court around which farm buildings are grouped. From there one comes to the residential part of the house. The entrance to the residential quarters is preceded by a suite consisting of a vestibulum and a large paved room. This unit, which is separated from the residential area, could have been either a guestroom or a reception hall, as in Building I. A small vestibulum has typically Nabatean doorpost capitals, which were decorated by depictions of a human face, a bull's head, and an amphora,[57] and leads into an inner paved court. In it is the already familiar L-shaped device, to which an additional arm was added on the west. The residential part of the house contains three rooms on the north and two smaller rooms on the east. All these rooms except one were unpaved and were possibly servants' lodgings, which is perhaps also indicated by the fact that all rooms on the ground level were interconnected by doors (the communicating openings were blocked by masonry in the Byzantine period, when more living space was needed). Below the rock floor of the east room in the north wing a 6-meter-deep cistern, with a capacity of 300 cubic meters, was excavated. The cistern, which has a rectangular opening, was fed from two sources. Rainwater on the flat roofs of the rooms around the court collected into a small pool and then flowed into the cistern via an underground channel. But most of the water was fed to the cistern by a hole outside (north) of the room, into which water brought from the dams in the wadis was poured. An entrance to a large storeroom is located at the southeast corner of the court. The south side of the court is occupied by a small, well-protected unit. It consists of a vestibulum leading on the west into a small room with thick walls and with a deep, low, arcuated entrance. Another door, in the east wall, leads into a staircase-tower of the Building II type. The whole court and some of the rooms around it were plastered and painted. The court was decorated with floral and geometric designs. Best preserved are the paintings in the vestibulum. The decoration consisted of two levels; a lower, narrow one and a wider one above. The lower level included geometric and carpetlike designs; and a representation of Eros and Psyche, identified by inscriptions in Greek. Only the Greek inscription remains of another small panel, in which a "good daemon" was represented. The upper level, less well preserved, included human figures, one of which is possibly a representation of Leda and the Swan. The arches—most of the segments of which were found in the debris—were decorated by figures of nude men and clothed women. The middle arch segments were decorated by a bust of a young man. One of the artists, Samuel, signed his name in Greek.

The upper level was reached by two staircase-towers, the one already mentioned, and the other situated at the west end of the court, which served the rooms in the north and east wings. At least one room on the north upper floor had a mosaic pavement—the only second-floor mosaic pavement of its time known in Palestine. The other staircase served only one room, presumably a strong room. At some time in the history of the house, at the end of the first

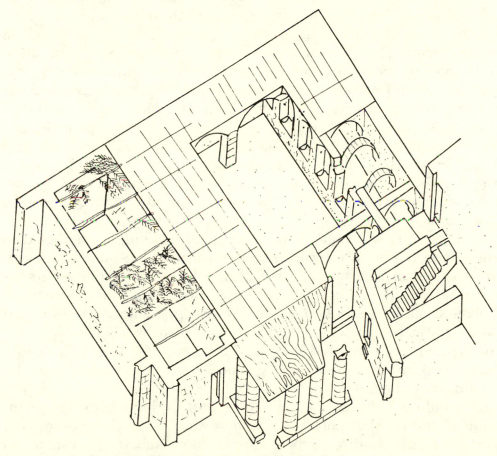

34. Mampsis: Building XII: the stable. (B. Brimer).

63

quarter of the third century C.E., the owners of the house, who evidently did not feel at ease, decided to find a better place to hide their most precious belongings, which consisted of a large bronze jar containing 10,500 dinars and tetradrachms. Thus, a hiding place was built under a landing in the strong room's staircase-tower, and the jar was deposited in it for safekeeping.[58] Indeed, the jar remained there until 1966, when it was discovered.

The part of the house adjoining the large court was only partly excavated. It contains a west wing of good masonry and a south wing with storerooms and workshops of lesser workmanship. To the east of the court is another stable, larger than the one in Building XI. It was also made in basilican form, but the central space was too large to be roofed with arches. Each of the two aisles contained an arched opening and six windows, which provided room for twenty-four horses in both aisles. There is evidence that at some time horses were also placed in the central space. Both aisles were joined by gangways resting on double arches at the east and west ends of the central space. There were probably covered porticoes above the aisles. The roofs of these porticoes were supported by column drums and building stones embellished by rosettes found in the debris. Access to these porticoes was given by an L-shaped device, the third discovered at Mampsis, in front of the stable. This device was made of a solid stylobate on which were placed five freestanding columns, with typically Nabatean capitals.[59] It supported a wooden balcony, access to which was given by a staircase-tower of the Building XI type. Prospective buyers probably admired the beautiful animals from the porticoes.

This staircase-tower led to another installation, unparalleled in the whole region: a most elaborately planned and built bathroom. It consisted of a vestibulum, which through a wide arch led to the bathroom itself. Against the back wall was a small stone structure, hollowed out in the middle; above this was apparently a large wooden stool. The tank below the stool was connected by a short pipe with an earthenware jar placed in a hole in the ground. The device could be flushed by water running in a pipe from a tank built against the wall outside the house.

Building XII was first built at the end of the first or the beginning of the second century C.E. Where this architecture originated is still a riddle. It differs from contemporary Nabatean construction in Auranitis. However, Mampsis seems to have been too small a site

64

to have served as a place where a school of architecture could develop independently. For the solution to this riddle we must, perhaps, await further excavations in the capital of the Nabatean Negev, Elusa.

Located in the vicinity of Building XII are the market building (Building IV), the public reservoir (Building VII), and the bathhouse (Building V). Building IV has been little excavated. It consists of two streets along which there are three rows of shops. Its east end was damaged when the monumental stairway leading to the large East Church was built, but from its west end we learned that there were doors by which this large building could be closed. It is identified as a market because the rooms were not interconnected and opened only on the streets. Building VII was originally labeled

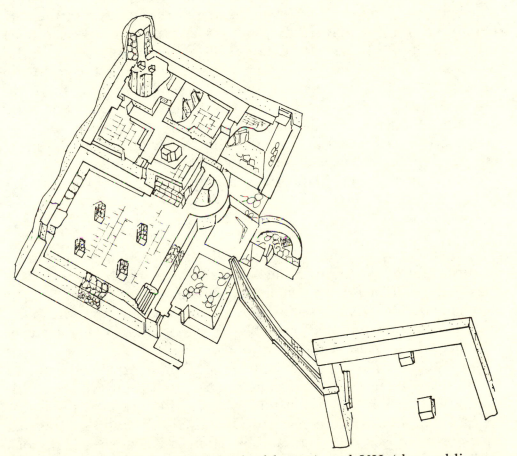

35. Mampsis. Buildings V (the bathhouse) and VII (the public reservoir). (B. Brimer).

a temple because of its west wall, which was built of large ashlars. It measures 10 by 8 meters and is 3 meters deep. At its east end is a small square tank, into which water brought from the wadi was poured to settle. When the city wall was built at about 300 C.E., a short conduit was added, leading water from an opening in the wall to this tank. Clean water from the tank flowed over the wall into the reservoir. The reservoir was roofed by arches springing out of the long walls and were supported by heavy piers built along the middle of the reservoir. At the reservoir's west end steps led down to make it possible to drain out the water to clean the reservoir. The entire structure was coated with excellent gray plaster, which is typical of the Nabatean period (reddish plaster, a result of the addition of ground pottery, was used in the Byzantine period). The quality of the builders, and their rich experience in the building of such structures, may be judged by small details (e.g., the rounding of the corners in such a way that cleaning the reservoir was made easier and the installation of a block of harder stone at the place where the water falls down from the settling tank to prevent damage to the plaster). In addition to serving as a reserve of water for the town, the reservoir also fed the nearby public bath (Building VII). The bathhouse consists of the usual components of a Roman bath: an apodyterium, a frigidarium, a tepidarium, a caldarium, and a heating device. The only difference between this and the type of bath used in Rome itself lay in the great care that was given to conserving water.

In this chapter I have attempted to describe some of the main features of a Nabatean town the construction of which began before the crucial date of 106 C.E., when the Nabateans came under Roman domination. The buildings at Mampsis, being an enterprise of twenty or thirty Nabatean families, possibly with no support from a central administration, yielded no inscriptions. At Oboda, however, which was a matter of public concern, the epigraphy is extremely rich. In Chapter I, I mentioned Nabatean-Aramaic inscriptions dealing with the agricultural activities that took place in the years 88 to 98 C.E. (p. 28). These activities continued after the annexation of Nabatea by the Roman Empire, as attested by Aramaic-Nabatean inscriptions of 107/8 and 126/27 C.E.[60] That these activities were still acquiring momentum in the third century C.E. is also attested by the large

66

number of Nabatean-Greek inscriptions found at Oboda.[61] What-ever the case might be at Petra, Nabatean Negev, and most probably also Nabatean Auranitis, owe their urbanization, not to the Romans, but to the Nabateans' own initiative.

Burial Customs
and Social Structure

In the previous chapter Strabo's companion's impressions of Nabatean funerary customs were cited: "They have the same regard for the dead as for dung, as Heracleitus says: 'Dead bodies are more fit to be cast out than dung'; and therefore they bury even their kings beside dung heaps" (*Geog.* XVI.2.26).

It was Kammerer who first paid attention to how little sense this statement makes: "Le reseignement le plus nettement erroné offert par Strabo à ses lecteurs, et celui touchant le mépris des cadavres et l'enfouissement scandaleux avec la voirie, de la dépouille des morts, fut-ce celle des rois. Les innombrables et majesteux tombeaux de ses valles, la tradition d'Obodas à Abdeh, où il fut divinisé, tout ce que nous savons de cette population, demontre qu'elle eut pour les morts un respect comparable seulement à celui pratiqué en Egypte. Cette hérésie de Strabon repose sur une sorte de calambour dépisté par Clermont-Ganneau: *kaphar* ou *kphar*, peut-être *kophra*, veut dire tombeau en araméen et en syriaque, et *kopron* en grec signifie fumier!"[1] Starcky, in his more recent work, in dealing with Nabatean

69

funerary customs, concluded: "Le culte des morts est encore attesté par les nombreuses nefesh sculptées dans le grès de Petra: nous avons déjà dit ce qui les caracterisait en tant que monument soulignons ici qu'en tant que mémorial et substitut du défunt, elles constituent un démenti à l'opinion de Strabon sur le mépris du cadavre qu'auraient manifesté les Nabatéens. . . . Un examen de la religion des Nabatéens devrait inclure une étude de leurs cérémonies et de leurs formules de prières. Espérons qu'ici comme d'autres domaines, les fouilles en cours permettons bientôt un bilan moins lacuneux."[2] The rather strange statement of Strabo was explained on different grounds by Wright,[3] who suggested that the Nabateans followed the funerary customs of the Bactrians, Sogdians, and Massagetae: "A comparative examination of these statements regarding the nomads of North-Eastern Iran leaves no doubt that what the classical authors were referring to (in a somewhat stereotyped fashion) is the Iranian practice of 'Ritual Exposure' of the dead; and it is difficult to avoid the conclusion that some such custom is posited

36. Petra. Partial view of the valley of Petra, showing the rock of Umm el-Biara with tombs at its base. (Elia Photo-Service, Jerusalem).

70

37. Petra. The main high place. Note the triclinia on the sides and the base for a statue in the middle.

for the Nabateans in Strabo 16.4.24." Further on, Wright suggests that some of the so-called high places, which abound at Petra, are nothing more than "exposure platforms." He also states that "among the Nabateans of Petra during the time when Athenodorus observed them, some group, class, or caste, exposed their dead in a way reminiscent of the Iranian manner. Since 'kings' are specifically mentioned, it may be that the practice was an aristocratic one." Wright is quite certainly correct. By exposing their dead long enough for the body to decompose, the clean bones could then be collected and placed in their permanent abode.

In any case, Nabatean burial customs stand out throughout the Semitic world and may be compared only with those of their contemporary Jewish neighbors. It is common knowledge that the Jews in the Second Temple period practiced two types of burial: direct burial, in which the remains of the body were never touched again, and a form of bone collection. In the latter case, the bones were removed from their original burial place. This could have been done

71

in the same family sepulcher in which the bones were moved from one chamber to another, or they could have been transported from a faraway country to a central cemetery, like the ones at Jaffa and Beth-Shearim. For a burial of the second type special containers were used, the most common ones being the stone ossuaries that have been found by the thousands in Jerusalem and its environs. This burial custom was the subject of a special study initiated by Meyers.[4] Meyers follows this custom, practiced in Palestine in two early periods—the Chalcolithic Age and the Second Temple period—throughout the ancient Mediterranean world. However, he omits one possible source for comparison, geographically the closest: the Nabateans.

Indeed, the Nabateans practiced both direct and second burial. In fact, as in the case of their Jewish neighbors, the second practice seems to have been more prevalant than the first. It is true that it is only natural for a visitor to Petra to pay most of his attention to the fascinating facades of the monuments, on which most of the studies have focused, and to ignore their interiors. Happily, the only thorough research made at Petra at the very end of the previous century, that of Brünnow and von Domaszewski, furnished enough material to make possible a review of the practice of second burial.[5] In addition to photographing, drawing plans, and describing the facades of the monuments at Petra, they also drew the plans and described numerous interiors of funerary monuments. The results of their research reveal the presence of monuments in which the sepulchral chambers are either empty or have very few loculi for an initial burial;[6] few have a considerable number of loculi.

In the more recent researches of the Horsfields a number of tombs were excavated, which, if their description is read carefully, may be explained in only one way—that they were used for second burials. Thus a tomb north of el-Habis: "No. 1 was a rounded narrow grave with shoulder pieces [apparently for cover stones] 0.60 m deep, filled to the brim with river gravel to a depth of 0.50 m, and then sand. The grave is so narrow that the corpse must have been forced into it, and it contained nothing but the skull and fragments of bone which have never been disturbed."[7] Of another tomb the Horsefields state: "The threshold grave, No. 4, was much wider. . . . Half-way down were parts of two skeletons side by side, the missing bones having disappeared through the silt. The tomb has been used as a charnel house, for beneath the top burials which

72

were orderly, were seven skulls and a mass of bones, piled up in confusion."[8] These are not the only tombs of this type at Petra. Little if any attention has been given to these descriptions.

Still more striking are the finds in the Nabatean necropolis at Egra. Here Jaussen and Savignac did excellent work in describing some seventy monuments and in photographing and drawing plans of interiors of a considerable number of tombs. At Egra the number of loculi in burial chambers is consistently larger than in those at Petra; but shallow niches of various sizes excavated in the walls of the burial chambers have also been observed at Egra. Of much interest in this respect is Tomb B 11, dated by an inscription to 58 C.E.[9] It has one large loculus excavated at ground level, apparently

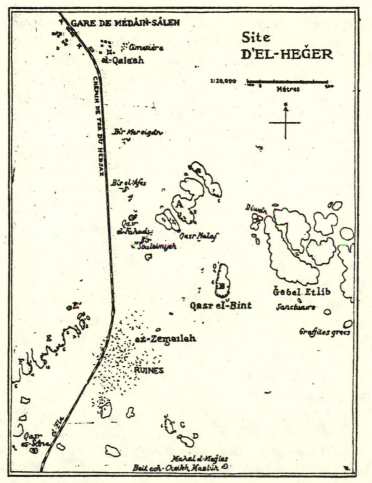

38. Egra. Plan of the site. (*Mission* I, Pl. I, Jaussen-Savignac).

for the burial of two persons. In addition to the loculus, six niches of different lengths were cut into the walls at different heights. None of these niches is deep enough to have contained a corpse. Another tomb, B 20,[10] has a similar arrangement of ordinary-sized loculi as well as shallow wall niches. Another tomb, A 3 (one of the earliest et Egra, dated to 4 c.e.), was more intricately arranged.[11] In this tomb, in addition to the usual loculi and the shallow niches in the walls of the chamber, there are niches in the loculi themselves. There was still another provision: in some tombs large repositories were cut deep below the floors of the loculi. Doubtless, these are similar to those found in the charnel houses at Petra referred to by the Horsfields. A typical tomb of this type is one named Qasr es-Sane.[12] In this tomb there are no ordinary loculi; instead, there are wall niches whose shape and size are not suitable for the deposition of a corpse. This is also the case in Tomb B 1, of 1 c.e.[13] In the magnificent monument B 4, named Qasr Abu el-Bint, made after 40 c.e.,[14] one can see how the shallow niches could be sealed by a slab of stone or a wooden board. Still of interest is the unique Tomb A 6,[15] consisting of one large hall (6 × 6 m), in three walls of which are loculi with troughs cut at their bottom. Each of these loculi is subdivided by thin partition walls into twelve square compartments (38–40 cm). Jaussen and Savignac suggested that these were used either for the burial of children or for the deposition of funerary urns. But these are too small even for children, and as far as is known the Nabateans never resorted to burning their dead. Thus, Petra and Egra furnish ample evidence of the practice of second burial by the Nabateans.

It is true that not a single relic of an ossuary was found in any of these tombs. However, the Nabateans could have deposited the bones of their dead directly into the above-described stone containers, or they could have followed the other Jewish custom of depositing bones into cedar wood ossuaries, which over a period of time would have disappeared without leaving any trace. In any case, the use of the Judean type of stone ossuary is still restricted to one case, described on p. 82. Another possibility is that the Nabatean ossuaries were of a type not used by other peoples, such as leather bags, which would disintegrate (of course, it is possible that some will be found in ideal conditions of preservation). The use of ossuaries made of such material may also help us understand why no remains of Nabatean burials of the early periods have yet been found.

74

In summing up the burial customs as reflected by the finds at Egra, the Nabatean burial practices seem to have been as follows: persons who died at home, mostly women and children, were initially buried in loculi in the family sepulcher. As the need for more burial space arose, as was the case in Judea, their bones were collected from the original grave and placed in receptacles underneath the loculi. Persons who died far away from home (e.g., while in a caravan or during a military campaign) were most probably interred in a temporary grave not far from where they died, and after an appropriate lapse of time their bones were probably collected and placed in a linen wrapper or a leather bag and brought to their final place of rest in the family sepulcher; their bones were probably deposited in the niches along the walls. These cemeteries were located in central places, such as Egra, where they were an integral part of a caravan halt, or in a place like Petra, a religious center. This explains why we find persons from Teima in the necropolis at Egra. That these were not chance burials we learn from the funerary inscriptions found at Egra, such as: "This is the tomb made by Wshuh daughter of Bagrat, and by Qayamu and Nashkuya her daughters, of Teima, for each of them, and for Amirat and Usranat, and Elanat their sisters, daughters of Wshuh and for their clients." And: "This the tomb and the base and the wall which were made by Hushabu son of Nafyu son of Alkuf from Teima, for himself and for his children and for Habu his mother, and Rufu and Aftiyu her sisters and her children."[16] This most probably also explains the presence of so many funerary monuments at Petra and why there is so little space for the living. Without taking into consideration the religious beliefs attached to the custom of second burial, for which there is no literary support, it is only natural that such a burial custom would develop in a society originating in a nomadic tribe.

If needed at all, the final proof for the Nabateans' practice of second burial comes from my excavations at Mampsis.[17] At Mampsis there were two basic forms of burial: direct burial and bone collection. Despite the fact that mountains with steep slopes suitable for the excavation of burial caves rise south and east of the city, the local Nabateans preferred the easier way of digging graves in the rather soft loessial plain to the north. Graves for permanent burial were dug in the ground in the form of holes measuring 1 by 2 meters and to a depth of 1 to 4 meters. The clad body was laid on its side, with an east–west orientation, the feet pointing to the east,

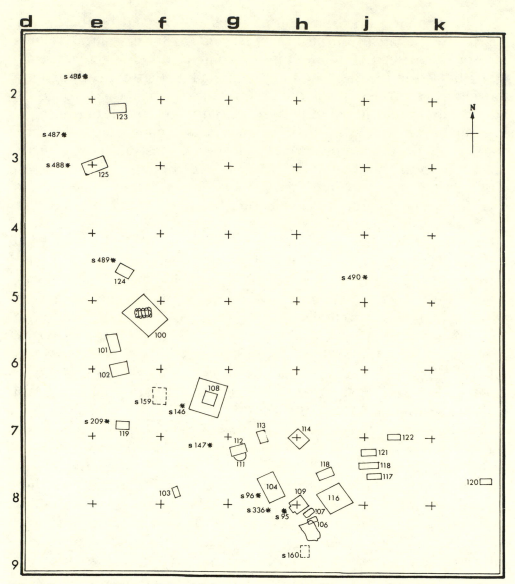

39. Mampsis. Plan of the Nabatean necropolis. Sites of funerary meals are indicated by the letter *S* and an asterisk. (A. Urweider).

the direction of the Nabatean religious center, Petra. Just as was prescribed by Jewish funeral customs, the body was laid on the bare ground and, in most cases, was placed in a coffin made of cedar wood; in rare cases no coffin was used. In most cases, the coffin was placed in a frame made of ashlars three courses high, which supported large flat cover stones (usually five). The rest of the shaft was

40. Mampsis. Partial view of the Nabatean necropolis showing Tomb 112 (that of a mother) and Tomb 111 (that of her child). Behind these are the remains of a table (marked 113) used at the funerary meal. (R. Brody).

then packed to the top with large fieldstones, wadi pebbles, and earth in order to make despoliation difficult. The dead were rarely deposited with any offerings—an alabaster jug formed in one tomb is an exception—but women were interred with their personal jewelry on them. Another exception are fragments of a small wooden box filled with documents, probably personal. This wooden box (this tomb, 107, has a very simple shaft, no coffin, and no stone structure) was (ritually?) burned at the feet of the deceased in the course of the

77

41. Mampsis. Tombs in the Nabatean necropolis. In the foreground is Tomb 118, with coverstones; in the background is Tomb 121, with base of the monument, fillings, and coverstones below. (R. Brody).

funeral. Almost all the tombs answering to this description were those of women, as is indicated by the jewelry found in such tombs. Denarii of Trajan were found in two of these sepulchers. The coins were placed in the mouths of the deceased as payment to Charon, keeper of the gates of the underworld. A monument, the *nephesh,* was built directly above the shaft. At the base of the monument a frame of ashlars with a filling of small stones and gravel laid in mortar was constructed. The base supported the monument in the form of a stepped pyramid. Such monuments were made of good ashlars, and their stones were stolen in antiquity, except in the case of Tomb 119, in which the filling of the shaft was not well made, so that the monument collapsed into it.

The form of second burial varied considerably. The most elaborate form was the large charnel house of Tomb 108. It consists of a base measuring 5.30 by 5.00 meters made of a triple row of ashlars and of two steps; its total width is about 1.00 meter. Within this

42. Mampsis. Remains of a funerary monument (Tomb 119), built in the form of a stepped pyramid, in the Nabatean necropolis. (R. Brody).

structure there was space for two chambers, but one only was completed. This chamber, oriented to the east, was built of ashlars, with a cobbled bottom, and is 2.20 meters long, 0.80 meters wide, and 1.60 meters deep. This charnel house was used in two separate periods. When a thin layer of topsoil was removed, two heaps were found; one was composed of several skulls, the other of the remaining bones. A jug of a well-known type of the third century C.E.[18] was in the center. There were also numerous coins of 308 C.E., the time of Diocletian, that had been left by the mourners. When these remains were removed, half a painted bowl of a familiar type was found,[19] along with two pottery lamps of the second half of the first century C.E. and later. Then came the usual five stones that covered the chamber. Numerous small fragments of human bones, teeth, many beads, half of a painted bowl, and a silver coin of Rabel II of 74 C.E. were found. All the stones of the upper part of the monument have disappeared, but since this charnel house was made for multiple use, it must have had a hollow structure.

43. Mampsis. Roman lamp of the second half of the first century
C.E. found in the Nabatean necropolis in the remains of a funerary
meal. (R. Brody).

Another type of second burial made use of stone-built boxes
that were placed on the surface of the ground.[20] These were made
of thin slabs of stone that were placed on their narrow sides and
covered by small stones, which formed a box. Two such boxes were
found. The interior measurements of the larger box are 1.85 by
0.45 by 0.35 meters; the smaller one measures 1.10 by 0.35 by 0.30
meters. Not only are they too shallow to accommodate complete
bodies, but in fact each box contained only a few bones, obviously
those of persons who were originally buried somewhere else. The
larger box contained several iron nails from the wooden coffin in

44. Mampsis. An ossuary (Tomb 109) in the Nabatean necropolis. (R. Brody).

which the person was initially buried; the other contained a golden earring of a very simple type. The third tomb, 105, was the most interesting form of second burial installation. Although it was discovered in September 1965, it was not excavated before June 5, 1967, a day before the outbreak of the Six-Day War.[21] Even before the excavation, one could see the base of a monument, made of ashlars and gravel filling, above the surface of the ground. At the southeast side of the frame there was an additional small frame; in it, in situ, was an uninscribed round-topped stele. As time went on, since my team and I did not fully understand the meaning of this structure, we took every precaution to study it without destroying it. Thus, we exposed the stone filling on all sides and drove narrow pipes into it in order to probe its interior. The approaching war forced us to excavate it as quickly as possible. When we removed the filling, we came upon a hole measuring 1.40 by 1.00 by 0.60 meters. In this hole we found a Judean type of ossuary made of stone, with a rounded but undecorated cover. In it was a bundle of bones packed in a cloth wrapper, which was brown when discovered. In the two opposite corners of the ossuary were two small glass phials, obviously for an odoriferous substance, again in accordance with Jewish funerary law relating to second burial. This Nabatean stone ossuary still remains unique. Additional proof of the Nabatean practice of second burial was furnished in 1979 at Elusa, where part of a family tomb was excavated.[22] Strangely, the monument was not built above the ground, as at Mampsis, but below it. It was made of fine ashlars to a depth of 1.80 meters, with a north–south orientation.

45. Mampsis. Tomb 105, which contained an ossuary, in the Nabatean necropolis. (A. Urweider).

Below the monument was a thick deposit of large stones and another of large wadi pebbles. At a depth of approximately 3 meters a stone-built sepulcher with an east–west orientation, covered by the usual cover stones, was found. In the middle of the sepulcher there lay a complete skull and a vertebra above it; the rest of the bones were scattered. If needed at all, this is conclusive proof that the Nabateans did indeed practice bone collection and second burial.

As we have seen (p. 79), the Nabateans' descendants practiced bone collection to as late as the beginning of the fourth century c.e. The only change in the two late tombs pertaining to this period is that their floor was covered by stone, and the structure of each resembled a pencase.[23] It seems that with the advent of Christianity at Mampsis by the middle of the fourth century the custom of bone collection was discontinued.

Nearer to Mampsis, northeast of the town, a second necropolis was discovered. The two Latin inscriptions found in it attest that it pertained to units of the Roman army stationed at Mampsis at the beginning of the second century c.e.[24] In this necropolis some ten

46. Mampsis. View of the Roman military necropolis looking north. (R. Brody).

47. Mampsis. Site of a pyre on which a soldier was cremated in the Roman military necropolis.

soldiers were incinerated on pyres. The pyre was set up on a flattened rock, and above the ashes a monument was placed, resembling either the Nabatean stepped pyramid or an elongated heap of large boulders. In no case is incineration associated with the Nabateans.

Strabo's statement, "They prepare meals in groups of thirteen persons" (XVI.4.26), is all that ancient classical literature offers on the subject of the common solemn meal practiced by the Nabateans.

84

Archaeology is much more generous, however. In a ritual held in the Nabatean temple a festive meal, in which the flesh of the victims was eaten, must have formed a very important component of Nabatean religious practices, as it did in Israel in biblical and postbiblical times. Except for the triclinia, which formed part of the open-air high places, special provisions were made for dining in the Nabatean temples themselves. Both the north and south wings of the temple at Khirbet et-Tannur contained rooms and halls of various sizes; in three of the smaller rooms in the northeast part and in the large hall in the south wing there were stone-built clinae, obviously meant for dining.[25] Glueck has alluded to the possibility that such triclinia were also provided in the Nabatean temple of Iram but has not produced more evidence from the Nabatean sphere. The Hauran (Auranitis) and the Ledja (Trachonitis) seem to offer more examples of triclinia. After studying the temple of Ṣaḥir,[26] I suggested that the rectangular theatron with covered porticoes and with benches along the walls was used as a dining hall for festive meals in the

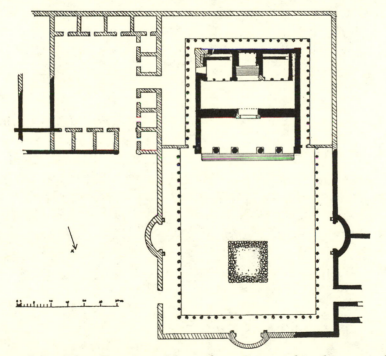

48. Petra. Qasr Bint Faraʿun. Note the rectangular theatron in front of the temple and the small rooms, possibly triclinia, on the southeast. Drawing by Mrs. Anat Negev-Palti (after Wiegand, *Petra*).

49. Petra. The Tomb of the Urn. The vaulted chambers support the forecourt. Dining places were probably located in the porticoes flanking the court.

summer and that in the winter the small theater (an odeum), with all probability a covered structure, was used for the same purpose. An arrangement similar to that of Khirbet et-Tannur probably existed in the large religious center of Seeia in Auranitis. The open-porticoed theatron was probably used in the summer, and the closed triclinia were probably located in the ruined structures north and south of the first and second terraces.[27] This also seems to have been the case at Petra. In the older plans of Qasr Bint Farᶜun, the city's main temple, the building is placed within a large temenos wall, at which are shown remains of halls[28] that probably enclosed the triclinia; the open-air theatron was probably located in the large court in front of the temple, in which a large altar was also discovered. Lamentably, no attention was paid to the subject of the sacred meal in any of the earlier researches.

That the funerary meal formed part of the ritual of the dead is clearly indicated by the finds at Petra. The Tomb of the Obelisks is

50. Petra. One of the two porticoes of the Tomb of the Urn.

located at the entrance to the *siq,* and the Bab es-Siq triclinium is nearby.[29] There are three wide clinae in its central chamber. Next comes the Khazneh, Petra's most famous monument, perhaps the burial place of Aretas IV. With all probability the central hall contained tombs, but the side chambers, which were not clean when the plans of this monument were drawn, possibly did not contain tombs, as suggested by Dalman, but may have served as triclinia. Another striking example is the triclinium of the so-called Tomb of the Roman Soldier.[30] The tomb, with its chambers on one side and a most elaborately made triclinium on the opposite side, all excavated in the living rock, are situated at the side of a huge triple portico. Thus, the open-air porticoes and the rock-cut-covered dining places may be compared with similar ones in Nabatean temples. In the Tomb of the Urn[31] the arrangement is somewhat different. In front of the huge tomb is a platform supported by a double row of vaulted halls. Deep rock-cut porticoes are located at both sides of the platform. These also were probably used as dining places for ritual meals.

87

51. Petra. The Tomb of the Obelisks. The entrance to the triclinium is on the upper level.

Different again was probably the arrangement in the Corinthian Tomb and the Palace Tomb.[32] In both there is a large burial hall, and at its flanks are three smaller chambers with no apparent burial places in them; these were probably used as triclinia. Last I shall mention the Turqmaniya Tomb, on the facade of which the only large Nabatean funerary inscription found at Petra is engraved.[33] This tomb consists of a large hall from which a narrow passageway leads into an equally large burial hall. The first hall was probably used as a triclinium. There may be a hidden reference to a triclinium in the large inscription, not all of which is clearly understood.[34] These are only few of the numerous rock-cut triclinia at Petra. Other dining places could also have been built in the open, in the vicinity of the tombs. The numerous cult niches, hundreds of which are scattered all over Petra[35] and Egra,[36] and some of which are located in partly covered rock shelters, could also have served as such family dining places.

Mampsis and Elusa furnish the clearest evidence of funerary

88

52. Petra. The Corinthian Tomb. The entrances on the left probably led to a triclinium.

meals. On the fringes of the Nabatean necropolis at Mampsis structures that are outwardly similar to the bases of funerary monuments were discovered.[37] These were identified as tables on which funerary meals were served. One, Table 101, measures 2.40 by 1.30 meters; another, Table 102, 2.25 by 2.35 meters. Tombs 100, 108, and 119 are located in the vicinity of these tables. Table 103, which measures 3.85 by 3.15 meters, is situated at the south end of the necropolis; the tombs pertaining to it have not been discovered. Farther north is Table 113, which was damaged when a new tomb, 112, was excavated near it. Heaps of broken pottery were discovered in the vicinity of these tables. These heaps are marked by the letter *S* on the plan of the necropolis.[38] The first heap, S 95, was discovered by chance when the area southwest of Tomb 105 was excavated. When a section was made through these remains, traces of a campfire were discovered and numerous pottery vessels were stacked in the ashes. This was one of the richest "suppers," as we then called them. It included casseroles, more than 100 simple dishes, small jugs, cups,

89

53. Egra. A rock-cut sanctuary (the Diwan) and triclinium in the midst of the necropolis.

a pottery lamp,[39] and parts of a large water jar. This funerary meal, in which many people participated, is dated to the second phase in the history of the necropolis (i.e., from the last quarter of the first century to about 150–200 C.E.).[40]

The remains of the earliest funerary meals, S 159 and S 146, were found in the vicinity of the charnel house in Tomb 108. The pottery[41] included early Roman Eastern Sigillata A vessels and a large variety of Nabatean painted bowls, which disappeared in the ensuing phases. Phase I is dated to the period between the last quarter of the first century B.C.E. to about the middle of the second century

90

54. Egra. A gabled cult niche with two stelae. Note the typical stone-dressing.

C.E. The coin of 74 C.E. found in Tomb 108 verifies this dating. However, the charnel house was used also in Phase III, and S 147 pertains to this phase.[42] In this phase Eastern Sigillata A became rare, and only one type of the Nabatean painted ware survives. This phenomenon of the use of the same structure throughout Phases I and II may also be observed in other parts of the Mampsis necropolis. However, pottery of Phase III (i.e., from the late third and the early fourth centuries C.E.) was found in S 485, S 488, and S 490, situated on the northwestern outskirts of the necropolis.[43] The pottery of these late funerary meals is completely different from the pottery of the earlier phases and has similarities to the pottery of northern Palestine and Phoenicia of the same period. Thus, the practice of the funerary meal extends over a period of more than 300 years. The fact that each of the funerary meals contained one or two lamps at the most signifies that the services were held during the day and that the kindling of light was a merely symbolic act. The pottery of all the funerary meals was intentionaly broken, and in S 95, in the vicinity of the ossuary tomb, 105, we even found the stone that was used to break the large heap of bowls lying on top of the heap of broken pottery. It seems that, as in Jewish funerary laws, vessels used in a cemetery were considered ritually unclean, and thus they were broken on the spot. Indeed, the Nabateans produced pottery of inferior quality for use in cemeteries. Funerary meals included olives, dates, fowl, and sheep.

Additional evidence comes from Elusa[44] where, in the middle of the cemetery, two triclinia built on the surface of the ground were discovered. These were made of unhewn fieldstones. In the vicinity of the triclinia a tower consisting of four rooms built below the ancient surface of the ground was found. One of these rooms served as a kitchen in which the food served in the cemetery was probably prepared; among other things found in the kitchen were baking ovens, cooking pots, and Nabatean painted pottery. No chronological conclusions concerning this cemetery have as yet been made, though the pottery scattered on the ground seems to be comparable to Phases I and II at Mampsis.

One of the most typical features of any given Nabatean site is the enormous quantities of pottery to be found. This fact needs some explanation, since it has some bearing on the subject treated here. Anyone who visits a site once occupied by the Nabateans is struck by the immense quantities of pottery strewn about on the surface of the site. The size of the city dumps, or "rubbish heaps," as they were called by some, has also been pointed out. At Petra the Horsfields excavated the Katute dump and dumps designated A–F.[45] Also, on their visit to Elusa, Woolley and Lawrence found it necessary to point out that "the size of the vast rubbish-heaps that surround the town points to its long life."[46] I was amazed by the size of the Nabatean dump that my team and I excavated at the beginning of my work at Oboda. We collected hundreds of thousands of pottery sherds from a rather small part of the dump. Some 20,000 pieces of the painted pottery were marked, as were more than 10,000 pieces of other types of pottery. The North Church at Oboda was built above a fill that contained immense quantities of pottery originally belonging to the Nabatean temple that once stood there. We also discovered a cave that was full of Nabatean pottery in the vicinity of the northeast tower of the late Roman-Byzantine citadel at Oboda. This richness is indicated also by the great number of types of pottery and by the varying quality of the wares. In no other period in the history of the region were so many types of pottery imported from abroad—from as far west as the Gallo-Belgian regions to eastern Egypt, the Crimea, and Asia Minor—and all this in a short period of time, beginning about 30 B.C.E. and ending not much later than 100 C.E. However, by the end of first century C.E. Nabatean pottery follows the style of an ordinary urban-rural society.

In studying the rich repertoire of pottery found at Oboda we learned that Nabatean pottery was produced in three qualities. When considering the best-known class of pottery (painted pottery), one may easily discern good-quality bowls made for use in the household; bowls of the same size and with almost the same kind of decoration but of lesser quality as far as ware and painting are concerned for use in cemeteries; and good-quality bowls that are half the size of ordinary household bowls for use in the temples. Strange as it may seem, at the turn of the millennium the Nabateans, who did not produce pottery before 50 B.C.E., made extensive use of it in households, in the temple, and in funeral services. Strabo's statement that "The king holds many drinking-bouts in magnificent style, but no one drinks more than eleven cupfuls, each time using a different golden cup" (XVI.4.26) is symptomatic. It is thus possible not only that the vessels used in funerary rituals were discarded but that those used in the temple were also discarded. The existence of summer and winter triclinia in the temples, and the presence of an enormous quantity of discarded pottery in cemeteries and temples, points to the importance the Nabateans attached to the solemn meal. The unusual quantities of pottery found at Nabatean sites only emphasize this fact.

If we take the excavation reports of Petra at face value, then the Nabateans supplied the dead with very few offerings, and even personal belongings, such as jewelry, were removed from them before burial took place. The Horsfields found little more than pottery in the tombs they excavated; the two bronze bells, the fragment of a silver bracelet, a child's bracelet of copper wire, a bronze bracelet, a bronze spherical bottle for oil, and a bronze ring are exceptions.[47] The yield of Murray's and Ellis's excavations was even poorer in finds other than pottery.[48] I am afraid that, in light of the excavations made in the Nabatean necropolis at Mampsis, the lack of finds of pottery at Petra is a result of the excavation procedures, not of Nabatean customs.

The yield at Mampsis consisted of women's personal jewelry. Thus, Tomb 100 yielded two tubular earrings, a decorated flat earring, and a dolphin pendant (similar dolphins came also from Tombs 118 and 121);[49] Tomb 107 contained a bell-shaped nose ring; Tomb 115 contained a pair of large tubular earrings and a rattle-shaped nose ring; in Tomb 119 there were one pair of dolphin earrings inlaid by semiprecious stones, one pair of larger crescent-shaped earrings, and a pendant; in Tomb 112 there were one pair of tubular earrings and a pair of flat earrings with a ruby inlay; and in Tomb 118 there were two pairs of earrings, a tubular one and another decorated by small shields and coiled wire (not to mention simple gold wire earrings found in other tombs). The only possible conclusion that one may draw from these finds is that women were interred with their jewelry.

The jewelry found at Mampsis provides a new field of study in Nabatean material culture.[50] Very few of the pieces are paralleled elsewhere. On the other hand, certain elements, like the wreath on the flat earrings, are found in Nabatean painted pottery and on capitals on the Nabatean temple at Oboda; the goddess ᵓAllat-Aphrodite standing in a shrine was found at Oboda in gold, in bronze, and on a pottery lamp; the pair of flat earrings, with two rubies, is believed to be a representation of the Nabatean goddess el-ʿUzza.[51] Figures of dolphins, five of which were found before Nelson Glueck published his monumental volume, *Deities and Dolphins,* are certainly Nabatean. With the help of these finds one will be now able to identify Nabatean jewelry that finds its way to the antiquities market. Other unique finds are those of Tomb 107. The bell-shaped nose ring has already been mentioned. At the feet of the woman buried in this tomb charred remains of a wooden box and oxidized pieces of copper hinges and lock were found, as well as a score of seal impressions on clay. An examination of the backs of the seals showed marks of papyrus and of a string by which the documents were bound.[52] The seal impressions come from official seals of Petra,

94

55. Mampsis. A seal impression made from a coin of Petra, 130 C.E., found in Tomb 107 of the Nabatean necropolis. (R. Brody).

56. Mampsis. An impression from the seal of Characmoba showing Tyche of Arabia, found in Tomb 107 of the Nabatean necropolis. (R. Brody).

95

57. Mampsis. An impression of the seal of Rabbathmoba, indicating the month of Maraxon (Marheshvan) and depicting Scorpio. It was found in Tomb 107 in the Nabatean necropolis. (R. Brody).

Rabbathmoba, and Characmoba. These impressions were dated by one seal that is a copy of a coin minted on the occasion of Hadrian's visit to Arabia in 130 C.E. The others bear various images of Tyche, such as those of Tyche seated on a rock, known only from coins struck at Petra during the time of Marcus Aurelius and Lucius Aurelius Verus and later; Tyche of Arabia, known from coins struck at Bostra, possibly in Hadrian's time; and Tyche seated on a stool, unknown from any other place. The gods are represented by a war god, known from coins of Characmoba, possibly from the time of Antoninus Pius, but certainly from the time of Septimius Severus, Julia Domna, and Geta. In another large group of seals signs of the Zodiac—are represented Libra, Scorpio, Saggitarius, possibly Capricorn, Aquarius—all pertaining to the winter. This is reminiscent of the arrangement of the signs of the Zodiac at Khirbet et-Tannur;[53] Glueck recognized their unusual disposition, according to which

96

58. Mampsis. An impression of a seal of Characmoba indicating the month of Xasleu (Chislew) and depicting Saggitarius. It was found in Tomb 107 of the Nabatean necropolis. (R. Brody).

the signs from Aries to Leo run counterclockwise on the head of the goddess and run clockwise from Libra to Pisces (to which our series of signs belongs). This unusual arrangement may have represented the two New Year feasts celebrated by the Nabateans, one in the spring, the other in the autumn. The seal impressions of Mampsis are thus of utmost importance for the study of numismatics of the Provincia Arabia, of geographical history (the evidence of these seal impressions points to the fact that the urbanization of Characmoba and Rabbathmoba could have occurred much earlier than is usually assumed), and of the history of Nabatean religious beliefs. In particular, the excavations in the Negev shed new light on the history of Nabatean religious practices.

Nabatean Afterglow:
The Negev and Sinai

Both scholars and popular writers have done much injustice to Nabatean history and archaeology. Although one may now trace Nabatean history and archaeology for a period of approximately 1,000 years, scholarly effort centers mainly on the rather short period of prosperity covering the last century B.E.C. and the following two centuries, leaving the periods of growth and decline in obscurity. Although there is some justification for the uncertainties concerning the earlier times, the evidence relating to the later periods has simply been overlooked. In this chapter I shall try to present some evidence pertinent to the earlier times and new evidence relating to the later periods.

In the Bible, Arabians the Arabs are mentioned in connection with the tribute paid by the kings of Arabia to Solomon (1 Kings 10:15; 2 Chron. 9:14). It is noteworthy that "the Arabs too brought him [Jehoshaphat] seven thousand seven hundred rams and seven thousand seven hundred he-goats" (2 Chron. 17:11). At least the reference to Solomonic times must relate to the kingdoms of southern Arabia. The Philistines and "the Arabs who lived near the Cushites" revolted against Joram (2 Chron. 21:16–17; 22:1). It is, however, not certain whether these references to the Arabs pertain to the times to which they were ascribed in the biblical narrative or to later times.[1] The allusions to Arabs in Isaiah and Jeremiah are authentic, as in "there no Arab shall pitch his tent, no shepherds fold their flocks" (Isa. 13:20) and in "like an Arab lurking in the desert" (Jer. 3:2).

The following allusion to the Arabs made by Herodotus relates to the period between these biblical passages, as does the description of Diodorus-Hieronymus on pages 1–3. In connection with Cambyses' march on Egypt, Herodotus writes: "There he found Cambyses prepared to set forth against Egypt, but in no doubt as to his march, how he should cross the waterless desert; so Phanes showed him what Amasis' condition [was] and how he should march; as to this he counselled Cambyses to send and ask the king of Arabians for a safe passage. Now the only manifest way of entry into Egypt is this. The road runs from Phoenice as far as the borders of the city of Cadytis [possibly Gaza], which belongs to the Syrians of Palestine, as it is called. From Cadytis (which, as I judge, is a city not much smaller than Sardis) to the city of Ienysus the seaports belong to the Arabians. . . . Now between Ienysus and the Casian mountain and the Serbonian marsh there lies a wide territory or as much as three days' journey, wondrous waterless. . . . But at this time, there was as yet no ready supply of water; wherefore Cambyses, hearing what was said by the stranger from Halicarnassus, sent messengers to the Arabian and asked and obtained safe conduct, giving and receiving from him pledges. There are no men who respect pledges more than the Arabians. . . . Having then pledged himself to the messengers who had come from Cambyses, the Arabian planned and did as I shall show: he filled camel-skins with water and loaded all his live camels with these; which done, he drove them into the waterless land and there awaited Cambyses' army. This is the most credible of the stories told; but I must relate the less credible tale also, since they tell it. There is a great river in Arabia called Corys, issuing into the sea called Red. From this river (it is said) the king of the Arabians carried water by a duct of sewn ox-hides of a length sufficient to reach to the dry country; and he had great tanks dug in that country to receive and keep the water. It is a twelve days' journey from the river to that desert. By three ducts (they say) he led the water to three separate places" (*History* III.5, 7–9).

100

The only possible way to connect these Arabians with the Nabateans is to read what Herodotus has to say about their religion: "They deem none other to be gods save Dionysus and Heavenly Aphrodite. . . . They call Dionysus, Orotalt, and Aphrodite, Alilat" (III.8). Kammerer, following Charles Clermont-Ganneau, sought to identify Orotalt (Orotal in other versions) with Dionysus-Dusares[2] and ʾAlilat with the Nabatean ʾAllat.[3] Starcky, on the other hand, prefers the identification offered long ago by Lidzbarski, who suggested identifying Orotal with the Arab deity Ruda, a divine name found in Palmyrene in the form of Arsu, but there is no certainty about the sex of this deity.[4] Whatever the case, there is general agreement that the Arabian deities mentioned by Herodotus are Nabatean ones, which helps in identifying those Arabs who occupied the region of northern Sinai in the sixth century B.C.E. as Nabateans. Another important point is the ability of these Arabs to procure water in a waterless region. Herodotus was more inclined to believe the story according to which the Arabs simply filled ox-hides and brought them to the meeting place with Cambyses' army, but he does not say where the water came from. The other story, about which he is dubious, tells of bringing water from the mysterious river Corys. It is interesting, however, that this water is stored in tanks. In any case, these Arabians are skilled water suppliers in the desert. This less believable story brings to mind what the Diodorus-Hieronymus account had to say about the water supply in the waterless region in which the Nabateans lived. Both sources use the same Greek name for this kind of country: ʾάνυδρος.

We may now turn again to Diodorus-Hieronymus: "It is their custom neither to sow corn, plant fruit-bearing trees, use wine, nor construct any house; if anyone is found acting contrary to this, death is his penalty. They follow this custom because they believe that those who possess these things are, in order to retain the use of them, easily compelled by the powerful to do their bidding" (Diod. XIX.94.3–4). One cannot but compare this passage with the biblical description of the Rechabites: "I set bowls full of wine and drinking-cups before the Rechabites and invited them to drink wine; but they said: 'We shall not drink wine, for our forefather Jonadab son of Rechab laid this command on us: "You shall never drink wine, neither you nor your children. You shall not build houses or sow seed or plant vineyards; you shall have none of these things. Instead you shall remain tent-dwellers all your lives, so that you may live long in the land where you are sojourners." We have honoured all the commands of our forefather Jonadab son of Rechab and have drunk no wine all our lives, neither we nor our wives, nor our sons, nor our daughters. We have not built houses to live in, nor have we possessed vineyards or sown fields. We have lived in tents, obeying and observing all the commands of our forefather Jonadab. But when Nebuchadnezzar king of Babylon invaded the land we said, "Come, let us go to Jerusalem before the advancing Chaldaean and Aramaean armies." And we have stayed in Jerusalem.' " (Jer. 35:5–11, in the NEB).

In both Jeremiah and Diodorus-Hieronymus nomadic tent dwellers are referred to. "These were Kenites who were connected by marriage with the ancestor of the Rechabites" (1 Chron. 2: 55). We shall not be far from the truth in assuming that the early Nabateans and the Kenites not only shared common taboos but also dwelt in the same region.[5] The taboos imposed on the Nabateans were well rooted in the part of the world in which they lived.

I return again and again to the problem of the remote origins of the Nabateans because of my uncertainty about this matter. The fact is that from the beginning of the Hellenistic period to about the end of the first century B.C.E., or even somewhat later, the Nabateans were the only Arabians known to have been in the region extending from northern Arabia to Auranitis on the north and the Negev and Sinai on the west. All the sources often confuse Nabateans with Arabs or Arabians. There must be a good reason for this confusion. Thus Diodorus-Hieronymus: "Now the eastern parts are inhabited by Arabs, who bear the name of Nabateans" (XIX.94.2): "While there are many Arabian tribes who use the desert as pasture, the Nabateans far surpass the others in wealth" (XIX.94.4). Strabo mostly uses "Nabateans" but states: "But I return to Eratosthenes who next sets forth his opinion concerning Arabia . . . and through the adjacent countries of the Arabian tribes, I mean the Nabateans and Chauloteans and the Agraeans" (*Geog*. XVI.4.2). Strabo regularly prefers to use the name Nabateans except for those cases in which he wants to point out their negative qualities, which according to him are features common to all Arabs: "for the Arabians are not very good warriors even on land, rather being hucksters and merchants, to say nothing of fighting at sea" (XVI.4.23).[6] Or: "This came to pass because Obodas, the king, did not care much about public affairs, and particularly military affairs (this is a trait common to all the Arabian kings), and because he put everything in the power of

102

Syllaeus" (XVI.4.24).[7] Josephus too uses both Nabateans and Arabs but prefers the latter name. When speaking of the sons of Ishmael, Josephus identifies the Nabateans with Nabaiotes, Ishmael's eldest son, and in enumerating all of them he concludes: "These occupied the whole country extending from the Euphrates to the Red Sea and called it Nabatene; and it is these who conferred their names on the Arabian nations and tribes in honour both of their own prowess and of the fame of Abraham" (*Jewish Antiquities* I.221).[8] Later in this work the Nabateans are mentioned in connection with the meeting with Judas Maccabaeus and Jonathan, his brother (*Jewish Antiquities* XII.335). In the later stages of the Hasmonaean uprising Jonathan sends his brother, John Gaddis, "to the Nabatean Arabs" (or just Nabateans) (*Jewish Antiquities* XIII.10–11); then Jonathan "turned back from there to Arabia and made war on the Nabateans" (*Jewish Antiquities* XIII.179); Nabatean Aretas was an ally of John Hyrcanus (*Jewish Antiquities* XIV.31–33.46.48); and lastly Gabinius set out against the Nabateans (*Jewish Antiquities* XIV.103). However, Josephus uses the names Arabs or Arabians much more often, for both the biblical and the postbiblical periods. I shall cite only a few examples. Thus is mentioned "Malchus, the Arab King" (*Jewish Antiquities* XIV.370–72), whose assistance Herod asked; Herod made war against the "Arabs" and the "Arab king" (*Jewish Antiquities* XV.107–120, 123),[9] and the ensuing conflicts were between Herod and the "Arabs." The name Nabateans is never used in these accounts, and their country is invariably named Arabia. Finally, the lost books of Glaucus, dealing with the Nabateans among other Arabian peoples and places, are named Ἀραβικοῖς, Ἀραβικη ἀρχαιολογία, and περὶ Ἀραβίας[10] and that of Uranius is named Ἀραβικοῖς.[11]

In reference to Ammanitis, the "Nabatean Arabs" are mentioned (Steph. Byz. 80.20). In speaking of Thamuda in his third book, Uranius remarks that it is a Nabatean place bordering the Arabs (Steph. Byz. 306.12–13). In referring to Syrmaion it is said that it is a valley situated between the nomads and the Nabateans (Steph. Byz. 593.13). Saraka is a region in Arabia next to the Nabateans (Steph. Byz. 536.3). The Salamians (*salama* = peace) are an Arabian people who got their name because of their alliance with the Nabateans (Steph. Byz. 550.12–13), but they themselves are nomads (Steph. Byz. 551.17). Medaba is a city of the Nabateans (Steph. Byz. 449.6). Oboda is a Nabatean place (Steph. Byz. 482.15). Stephanus usually distinguishes between Arabia and Arabia Felix, and

103

thus Saua is a village in Arabia Felix, and another Saua is a city in Arabia (Steph. Byz. 558.5–6). However, Arabia is in no way identical with Nabatea, and here and there Nabatean cities are listed along with Arabian cities and places that are in Syria and in other countries in the region.

It is thus quite clear that from early times, perhaps from the Assyrian period, the region under discussion was inhabited by Arabs who from the fourth century B.C.E. were known to the classical authors by the name of Nabateans. It is, however, much more difficult to explain how the transition from their totally nomadic way of life in the Early Nabatean period to their sedentary life in the following stages in their history occurred. I can explain this transition only by differentiating concentric nomadism, which is based on a natural permanent source of water, from linear nomadism, at which stage the nomads were able to reach the Mediterranean coast. This was made possible by acquiring the ability to procure water in regions in which there were no permanent sources of water. Diodorus-Hieronymus depicts the Nabateans as being at a well-advanced stage of development. Herodotus, referring to events that occurred two centuries earlier, also found it necessary to point out the Arabians' skill in finding water in a waterless country. This was done either in a primitive way, that is, by transporting water from a permanent source (which is not mentioned in his account) or by a nearly incredible way, that is, by channeling the water of the river Corys by means of an oxhide aqueduct a distance equivalent to a twelve-day journey through the desert. Probably the only kernel of truth in this story is the great tanks ($\delta\epsilon\xi\alpha\mu\epsilon\nu\alpha\varsigma$, which could also be cisterns) in which the water was kept. Should we accept the other possibility, then these Arabians (Nabateans?) of the late sixth century B.C.E. would have been in an advanced stage of development, not much less than that of the early Hellenistic period. The Nabateans could have learned how to do this only in the lands of southern Arabia. The conditions of precipitation are not much different in southern Arabia from those in the Negev. On the southern coast the annual rainfall ranges between 1.6 inches (approximately that at Eilat) to 3.8 inches (less than at Oboda). Mukeiras in the higher mountains rising above the southern coast has an average of 9.5 inches, approximately that at Beersheba.[12] Agriculture was based on the occurrence of flash floods, and water for drinking was stored in cisterns. The connections between the Nabateans and the southern cultures are still a matter for

104

future research, although it is most likely that the Nabateans, the only nomadic tribe in that region that was able to procure drinking water, acquired their skill in southern Arabia.

In the previous chapters the anomalies in the development of Nabatean culture as reflected in urbanism, architecture, and ceramics were pointed out. Urbanism developed from encampments in the early stages, to encampments and the solid architecture of temples, caravanseries, and military installations in the Middle Nabatean period, and finally to the normal urbanism of a rural-urban society in the Late Nabatean period.

We do not know how the early encampments were organized. Knowledge of their very existence is still based on the single discovery of a tent site at Oboda. Oboda also offers much information about the organization of a large caravan halt of the Middle Nabatean period.[13] The magnificent temple was built on the western spur of an acropolis hill. The large military camp was located on the hill's northern side, whereas the roughly built enclosures, which I believe were made for camel breeding, were located at the southern side of the hill.[14] The only structures discovered between the military camp and the camel sheds were a khan of the third and fourth centuries and a farmhouse of the fourth and fifth centuries C.E. Remains of a campsite of the Middle Nabatean period have also been observed to the east of the Nabatean military camp. This is the best-known Middle Nabatean caravan halt in the Negev. The disposition of these elements at Nessana seems to have been similar to that at Oboda.[15]

In the first two stages of their history the Nabateans dealt solely in the spice trade (except for the side "occupation" of robbery). The loss of trade by the middle of the first century C.E. compelled them to turn to agriculture. Faithful to their ancestral taboos of not building, planting, and drinking wine, the Nabateans turned to the trade of horse breeding, which may be considered a small step from camel breeding, which they had practiced for hundreds of years. Evidence for this are the stables found at Mampsis, Oboda, and Sobata in the Negev and the still more numerous horse stables in the Hauran. We do not know which horse was bred in these regions, but it is likely that it was the famous northern African horse that was used in ancient times by the Egyptians, who also exported it to ancient Israel (see, e.g., Exod. 14:9; 1 Kings 5:6; 1 Kings 10:29). In addition to the

105

59. A Nabatean clay figurine of a camel. (Courtesy of Israel Museum).

stables, rock engravings of horses with Nabatean inscriptions were found at Wadi Mukatteb in southern Sinai. One of these engravings depicts a trotting horse being ridden by a man; another depicts a horse being led by a rope.[16] These engravings are of the second and third centuries C.E. At Oboda a mare ridden without a saddle and a beautifully made colt were drawn with a thin point of wet plaster on the wall of a tower built in 294 C.E.[17] At Petra and other Nabatean sites clay figurines of saddled horses with trappings were found, identified by the Horsefields as Nabatean.[18] Numerous similar figurines were found both in the potter's workshop and in the Nabatean dump at Oboda.[19] The introduction of horse breeding seems to have been the secret of Nabatean prosperity in the Negev (and other parts of the Nabatean kingdom) for the next 600 years.

The evidence for the beginning of this new age comes from

106

Oboda. On the acropolis of Oboda itself and in two valleys, one situated two kilometers south of Oboda and another situated some four kilometers southwest of the city, eight large stone objects, which I identified as libation altars, were discovered. Nabatean inscriptions were engraved[20] on one or more sides of these large stone objects. The longest of these inscriptions reads: "This dam [which was built] by . . . the sons of . . . / [and his associates] the sons of Saruta for the offering of sacrifices / to Dushara the God of Gaia in the year 18[?] . . . of the King Rabel king of the Nabateans who brought life and deliverance to his people."[21] The translation of the second word of this inscription was contested by Naveh[22] and Eissfeldt[23] (as were some other translations). Whatever the correct translation of this word is, the fact remains that between the eighteenth and the twenty-eighth regnal years of Rabel II (88/89–98/99 C.E.) the Nabateans underwent a revolution in their way of life. This revolution was so important that it called for special religious festivities, and it was probably in this connection that King Rabel was honored by the words "[he] who brought life and deliverance to his people." These words are also known from an inscription found at Petra and from four inscriptions from the Hauran, but none of these is earlier than 93/94 C.E.[24] The stables discovered at Mampsis, Sobata, and Oboda contain evidence of the importance of Rabel's activities. The impact of these economic activities in the Nabatean Negev was so strong that the Roman Empire's annexation of the Nabatean kingdom and the formation of the new province of Arabia, into which it was incorporated, had little effect on the life of the Nabateans; and, if any, it must have been positive. This one clearly learns from two Nabatean inscriptions, of 107/8 and 126/27 C.E., found at Oboda.[25] A Nabatean inscription found in 1979 in the midst of large farms some three kilometers north of Oboda, above the gorge of Nahal Zin, probably pertains to the same period. It reads: "Remembered for good . . . in front of Godly Obodas; and remembered / . . . [who made] . . . / Garm'allahi son of Thaim'allahi a statue in front of Godly Obodas / and he makes [this thing] not [for] benefit and not [for] any advantage / and if Death claims us, [I] shall not / be claimed; and if there will be any injury around, it shall not be around us / Garm'allahi wrote with his own hand."[26]

The apotheosis of Obodas, apparently Obodas II who ruled in the years 30 to 9 B.C.E., is known from an inscription found at Petra, dated to the twenty-ninth year of Aretas IV (20 C.E.). This inscription too speaks of a statue of Obodas the God.[27] The second inscription from Petra, undated, was written by a man named ʿObaidu, son of Waqihel, "and his associates of Obodas the God."[28] The term "his associates," translated "symposium" by Cantineau, is also found in three inscriptions engraved on the stone altars at Oboda.[29] Obodas's deification is also mentioned by Uranius in his fourth book: "Oboda, a settlement of Nabateans. Uranius [says] in his fourth book [that] there King Obodas, who has been deified, is buried there" (Steph. Byz. 482.15–16). We do not know whether Obodas was worshiped in the first Nabatean temple built in the city of Oboda, most probably named after him, but he was definitely venerated in the temple of Oboda that was rededicated in the third century c.e. But, before turning to this subject, we must return to the inscription from Oboda found in 1979.

It is now accepted by all scholars that the Nabateans originated in Arabia. If needed at all, then this is proved beyond any doubt by the analysis of Nabatean personal names presented in Chapter I.

60. Oboda. Greco-Nabatean inscription from the acropolis. It reads, in part: "To God Obodas . . . son of Kasiseos, Almaairos." (N. Suffrin).

108

But what was the language by which the Nabateans communicated? Was their written language, Nabatean-Aramaic, also their spoken language? Diodorus-Hieronymus states that "to Antigonus they wrote a letter in Syrian characters" (XIX.96.1). Indeed, they used this language for writing for about 600 years until it yielded completely to the Greek language by the beginning of the third century c.e. An inscription of 328 c.e. found at en-Nemara in the Hauran was written in Nabatean-Aramaic characters but in the Arabic language.[30] The inscription discovered near Oboda in 1979, although written in Nabatean, is in fact a bilingual inscription. The first three lines, in which the dedication of the statue to Obodas is expressed, were written in Nabatean-Aramaic, as is the last line, which contains the signature of the writer. On the other hand, the two lines that contain the declaration and disclaimer of the writer were written purely in Arabic. Is this the language the Nabateans spoke? Did the writer use this language because he could not find appropriate words to express himself in Nabatean-Aramaic?

Owing to the ruinous state of the Nabatean temple of Oboda (it served as a stone quarry for the construction of churches from the mid-fourth century on), the only way to distinguish between the two phases in its construction is to analyze the rich epigraphic material discovered on the acropolis hill. Several dedicatory inscriptions were discovered in the southwest staircase-tower of the temple. The longest one mentions Obodat, Phaṣa'el, and Sa'udat, sons of Ḥaretat.[31] A smaller fragment of an inscription found in the same location mentions year 2 of Aretas IV.[32] On the northeast gate is another dedication from the time of Aretas IV,[33] and finally a large building block has a dedication made by Ausos, son of Ghanmu.[34] All the dedications of the second phase of the temple were in Greek. Eight inscriptions were engraved on one lintel found in the debris of the portal leading from the portico to the shrine.[35] In a tabula ansata in the center of the lintel there are two inscriptions. One mentions Zamnos, the architect; the other refers to Soaidos and to the year 162 a.e. (Arabian era), or 267/68 c.e.[36] To the left of the tabula ansata is a wreath in which there is a dedication made by Nakebos.[37] The wreath on the right of the tabula apparently contained a dedication to Obodas.[38] Ausos[39] was mentioned on the upper border, and on the lower are the words "All friends of Oboda."[40] A column drum found in the debris of the portico has a dedication made by Raisos, son of Abdalgos, who built the roof of the temple or the

109

61. Oboda. Half of the lintel of the Greco-Roman-Nabatean temple. Part of the tabula ansata reads: "Let be remembered Zamnos the architect."

portico.[41] There are also several building stones with other dedications. One inscription[42] mentions the names of Abdomanos, Abdomaios, Souaidos, Ouallos, and Saadallas. On the other stone the names of Ammos, the architect, and Chasetos, son of Garamos,[43] are inscribed. Another dedication is made by Kaseisos and Almaairos. In a tower in the late Roman-Byzantine citadel was found the important inscription in which it is stated that "for the sake of piety and by the initiative of Ausoebdos son of Erasos was made the facing of marble of [the house of?] Aphrodite." It was built by Abdaiseos and Ameos, the architect, "out of their own resources."[44] Finally, an inscription discovered at the beginning of the century by Musil[45] speaks of the construction of the "tower" in 188 A.E. (293/94 C.E.) by Eirenaios, with the assistance of the architect Ouaelos from Petra and of Eutyches.

These were the inhabitants of Oboda in the third century who rededicated the old temple. The personal names are almost all Nabatean, and the few that are not may be explained quite easily. Some of the names are common and some are rare. Zamnos is Zamin, known only once in NA;[46] Soaidos pertains to a group of very common Nabatean names, found in various forms in different parts of the Nabatean realm;[47] Naqebos is Naqibu, found in NA and SEN,[48] and is also the name of a Nabatean general;[49] Ausos is one of the commonest Nabatean names (found 241 times in SEN);[50] Raisos is rare—it is either Rishu or Rasi (both are unique);[51] Abdalgos, on the other hand, is common;[52] Abdomanos is a rather rare name, occurring in EM and the H only;[53] Abdomaios, Abdomayu, is new

110

in this form; Ouallos is again one of the commonest Nabatean names (found 409 times in SEN);[54] Saadallos is a name common in all four regions but occurs mainly in SEN;[55] Ammos is very common (83 times in SEN);[56] Chasetos is very rare in Nabatean (once in NA but very common in Safaitic);[57] Garamos is common;[58] Kaseisos is not known in SEN but is common in the H, where it came from Safaitic;[59] Almaairos is common in all four regions;[60] Ausoebdos is found only once in EM;[61] Erasos is very common in SEN only (89 times); Abdaiseos is rare,[62] Ameos is very common in SEN (289 times.[63] We are thus left with the names Eirenaios and Eutyches. These are obviously Greek names, but in this context they may well be translations into Greek of good Nabatean personal names. The first name, from Eirene, "peace," is possibly Shalmu in Nabatean, a name common in all four regions;[64] Eutyches, "good Tyche," "good luck," is Gad-tab in Nabatean, a rather rare name.[65] These names manifest clearly who the inhabitants of Oboda were in the late Roman period. The only change that occurred in these inscriptions is that in the last century that elapsed from the time of the latest Nabatean inscription at Oboda (126 c.e.) to the beginning of the third century c.e. a cultural change came about, expressed by the use of the Greek language, which replaced the Nabatean language. As we shall see later on, the Nabatean language persisted only in remote southern Sinai to the very end of the third century c.e.

In dealing with these Greek inscriptions I left out the opening lines, which will be discussed now. Two opening formulas were employed:[66] $\Theta\epsilon\tilde{\omega}$ $\,{}^{\prime}$Óβο$\delta\alpha$, and the more common one, $Z\epsilon\tilde{\upsilon}$ $\,{}^{\prime}$Οβο$\delta\alpha$.[67] When publishing these inscriptions I concluded: "I doubt very much whether the veneration of King Obodas II survived in the second half of the third century c.e., three centuries after his apotheosis, and a century and a half after the annexation of his kingdom to the Roman empire. Such a suggestion must be based on more substantial evidence. I suggest that this inscription, as well as the others, in which Zeus Oboda is mentioned, refers to a local Zeus, the God of the town of Oboda."[68] How wrong I was and how right was Alt, who concluded from inscription no. 13 that a cult of Obodas did persist.[69] If more substantial evidence is needed, it is provided by the inscription discovered in 1979, mentioned earlier, of about one century earlier that mentions "Godly Obodas" twice. Whether the cult of the deified Obodas replaced the cult of Dushara completely, or whether these cults were amalgamated, is not known. The Na-

111

batean inscriptions of the last quarter of the first century C.E. found at Oboda mention only Dushara, and it is possible that the loss of political independence, on one hand, and the building of a new life at Oboda, on the other, were among the causes of a renewal of the older cult of King Obodas, after whom the city was named and, according to Uranius's account, in which his tomb was located. The goddess who was venerated, Aphrodite, is mentioned once at Oboda in connection with the facing, or paving (πλακωσις), of her house with marble. ʾAllat has long been identified with other goddesses, and one of these was Aphrodite.[70] She was also venerated in the old temple, and her image on a gold plaque, on a bronze figurine, and on a pottery lamp—all in the typical form of Venus-Aphrodite—were discovered in the temple's treasury.

As it did in other parts of Arabia, the cult of Apis penetrated Oboda also, as evidenced by a short dedicatory inscription engraved on a large building block of a wall of the North Church.[71]

The persistence of Nabatean culture may also be noted in the architecture of the third century C.E. at Oboda. At this time a new quarter was built south of the acropolis hill.[72] In this small quarter there were not more than ten houses, each built around a fairly large rectangular court. During a survey I made there I discovered remains of a peristyle in one of these houses. Only one building has fully been excavated and is identified by the inscription on its lintel as a *pyrgos* (tower), which indeed it is.[73] It was built with fine ashlars and has the same measurements of Late Nabatean Building II of Mampsis, but the arrangement of the rooms is different. A vestibulum leads into one hall in which the arches and the roof slabs were preserved intact. A narrow storeroom and a staircase-tower of the old Nabatean type leads to two upper floors. Were it not for the inscription that dates the building to 293/94 C.E.,[74] it could easily have been mistaken for an early-second-century C.E. Nabatean tower. The staircase-tower of this building is the latest-dated structure of this kind in the Negev. It gives way to a simpler form of staircase in the fourth century C.E.

The town of Mampsis assumed its present form in the second century C.E. No inscriptions were discovered at Mampsis that would permit the study of the transition from one Nabatean phase to another. However, the continuous use of the cemetery to the beginning of the fourth century may serve as evidence that the Nabateans occupied Mampsis throughout the Roman period. Although the lo-

112

cation of Late Nabatean Sobata is known, no excavations were made in the Nabatean part of the town, except for a house with two stables near the double reservoir. The history of Nessana in the late Roman period may be studied only from coin finds.[75] The coins, which apparently are only from the acropolis area, indicate some occupation of the site in the times of Septimius Severus (193–211), Galienus (253–68), Aurelian (270–75), Licinius (307–24), and Constantine (333–35). The excavations at Elusa are still at their beginning, and Libanius's letters are a better tool for the study of Elusa in the fourth century C.E. than is archaeology.[76]

Before turning to the next major stage in the history and archaeology of the Nabateans in the Negev, I wish to review the history of the Nabateans in Sinai. Although not borne out by any of the ancient sources, none of which identifies the native inhabitants of Sinai with either Arabians or Nabateans, the later history of Sinai is closely connected with the Nabateans. Drawing probably on Agatarchides,[77] the Diodorus-Hieronymus account states: "But we shall now take up the other side, namely, the opposite shore which forms the coast of Arabia, and shall describe it, beginning with the innermost recess. This bears the name of Poseidium,[78] since an altar was erected here to Poseidon Pelagius by that Ariston who was dispatched by Ptolemy to investigate the coast of Arabia as far as the ocean. Directly after the innermost recess is a region along the sea which is especially honoured by the natives because of the advantage which accrues from it to them. It is called the palm-grove and contains a multitude of trees of this kind which are exceedingly fruitful and contribute in an unusual degree to enjoyment and luxury. But all the country round about is lacking in springs of water and is fiery hot because it slopes to the south; accordingly it was a natural thing that the barbarians made sacred the place which was full of trees and, lying as it did in the midst of a region utterly desolate, supplied their food. And indeed not a few springs and streams of water gush forth there, which do not yield to snow and coldness; and these make the land on both sides of them green and altogether pleasing. Moreover, an altar is there built of hard stones and very old in years, bearing an inscription in ancient letters of an unknown tongue. . . . After sailing past the Palm-grove one comes to an island off a promontory of the mainland which bears the name Island of Phocae

113

from the animals which make their home there. . . . And the promontory which stretches out in front of the island lies over against Petra, as it is called, and Palestine, for to this country, as it is reported, both the Gherraeans and Minaeans convey from upper Arabia, as it is called, both the frankincense and the other aromatic wares" (III.42.1–5).[79]

There is no doubt that the springs and the large palm grove that are described are those later known as the oasis of Feiran, which the Nabateans must have known by the biblical name of Paran, which also occupied a very important place in the early history of Israel (see, e.g., Num. 10:12, 12:16, 13:26; Deut. 1:1; 33:2). This palm grove still forms an important source of livelihood for the Bedouin population of southern Sinai. The old stone altar and the ancient letters perhaps refer to the large Egyptian shrine at Serabit el-Khadem, at which there are numerous stelae of red granite inscribed with hieroglyphic texts.

The following description of Diodorus-Hieronymus puts the previous quotation in its correct geographical setting: "After one has sailed past this country the Laeanites Gulf comes next, about which are many inhabited villages of Arabs who are known as Nabateans. This tribe occupies a large part of the coast and not a little of the country which stretches inland, and it has a people beyond telling and flocks and herds in multitude beyond belief. Now in ancient times these men observed justice and were content with the food which they received from their flocks, but later, after the kings of Alexandria had made the ways of the sea navigable for their merchants, these Arabs not only attacked the shipwrecked, but fitting out pirate ships preyed upon the voyagers, imitating in their practice the savage and lawless ways of the Tauri of the Pontus; some time afterwards, however, they were caught on the high seas by some quadriremes and punished as they deserved" (III.43.4). The Laeanitic Gulf is usually emended to Aelanitic, but this is unnecessary, because the Nabateans were preceded in northern Arabia by the tribe of the Lihyanites, who later became their allies, as may be inferred from two inscriptions from Egra, written in Nabatean as "Masʿudu king of Lihyan," and the name of the gulf as given by Diodorus's source may be the correct old name.

Strabo (XVI.4.18) describes the same region in much the same words, naming Agatarchides as his source. He names the gulf "Aelanites" and the Nabateans "Nabatean Arabians." It was Pliny the

114

Elder who knew this gulf by its new name, Aelaniticus sinus (*Natural History* V.65), which possibly originated in the Roman period.

If it was not inhabited by Nabateans in the Hellenistic period, Sinai became Nabatean in the Middle Nabatean period. Pottery typical of this period has been found at Wadi Haggag.[80] It is, however, the Late Nabatean period that is best documented in southern Sinai. It is true that there are only a handful of dated inscriptions among the total number of approximately 4,000 inscriptions,[81] but it seems that all the other inscriptions fall between 150/51 c.e. (the date of the earliest-dated inscription) and 266/67 c.e. (the date of the latest). The Sinaitic inscriptions are dated according to the Arabian era, which is indicated by one inscription found at Wadi Mukatteb that says: "Year one hundred and six which equals the days of the three Caesars" (*CIS* II.1.963). This could only have been the year 211 c.e., when Septimius Severus died and Caracalla and Geta were Caesars. In this way Sinai together with the Negev and the rest of the Provincia Arabia dated their inscriptions by the Arabian era.

What is more important, however, is that at about the same time at which the Nabatean gave way to the Greek language in the Negev and the other districts of the former Nabatean kingdom, it enjoyed a renaissance in southern Sinai. Numerous attempts have been offered to explain why the Nabateans wrote their inscriptions on the rocks of southern Sinai.[82] None is satisfactory, however, so that Cantineau was forced to conclude: "En fait la question de l'origine des graffites sinaïtiques n'est pas éclaircie. Seul un examen très attentif des lieux pourrait peut-être la résoudre."[83] I have followed Cantineau's advice and have spent many days in Sinai attempting to find the system that lies behind this phenomenon. It is true that these inscriptions are found along the routes that cross the southern part of the peninsula from east to west and from north to south, on which Nabatean caravaners traveled, as suggested by Euting;[84] but they are also found in other places, such as faraway valleys, side wadis, mountain slopes, and mountaintops—in fact, everywhere in this part of Sinai. Some were written by highly skilled scribes and priests, as may be learned from numerous texts; others were crudely scribbled by shepherds who could not spell much more than their own names, and sometimes did not know how to write their fathers' names (usually found on Sinaitic inscriptions). That this region was not isolated may be inferred from a considerable number of bilingual (Nabatean-Greek) inscriptions.[85]

In Chapter I, I showed that the study of personal names attests the existence of a local population whose members derived their livelihood from the resources that the southern part of this arid peninsula offered. We thus find people occupied in cultivating date palms, weaving yarn, exploiting the copper and turquoise mines, hunting, and perhaps also engaging in some kind of caravan trade. The fact that Sinaitic inscriptions usually contain both the writer's and his father's names, and quite often those of his grandfather and his brothers, enables us to trace the genealogy of some families over a period of two, three, and even four generations. We thus often find at Wadi Haggag, which lies in the eastern part of the peninsula, names of people who also left their names at Jebel Musa, Wadi Naseb (the copper smelting region), Wadi Feiran, and Wadi Mukatteb, which lie in the center and the west of the region.[86] Others seem never to have left this important caravan halt.[87] Not only did the Nabateans in Sinai retain their original language; they also led very active religious lives. Moritz,[88] after dismissing all other hypotheses concerning the Sinaitic inscriptions, suggested that these are concentrated mainly in two regions—Jebel Musa (identified by some as Mount Sinai) and Jebel Serbal, rising above the valley of Feiran—which, according to Moritz, were sacred not only to Jews but also to the Nabateans. According to him, however, it was not local people but pilgrims from Hegaz who came to venerate their god at holy places in Sinai and wrote their names there. Moritz was right in only one thing: there were holy places in Sinai, but these pertained to the local Nabatean inhabitants of southern Sinai.

As mentioned earlier, as in other parts of the Nabatean realm, the Nabatean-Aramaic script was never used in connection with profane matters. All long texts known from elsewhere are either dedications of temples or are funerary inscriptions. I believe that even the short graffiti, many of which have also been found at Egra and its vicinity as well as at Petra, and in the thousands in Sinai, are all invocations.[89] Many of these inscriptions contain an opening, a closing, or both, of short invocations, and not a few of them were indeed written—as suggested by Moritz—by pilgrims on their way to visit the holy places. Nowhere in the Nabatean realm is such a large number of deities mentioned as in southern Sinai (see p. 9). In addition, none of the temples scattered throughout the Nabatean realm has offered a better understanding of temple administration than Jebel Moneijah in southern Sinai.[90] The local Bedouins call this

116

2,508-foot-high mountain The Mountain of the Conference of Moses. It is situated southeast of the oasis of Feiran, which overlooks the confluence of three of Sinai's major wadis. To the south rises Jebel Serbal (6,734 feet); to the north, Jebel el-Banat (4,017 feet). To this day, the Bedouins, especially the shepherdesses, perform a ritual at a small shrine on the top of the mountain; the ritual is connected with the fertility of their flocks, whom they put under the patronage of the ancient shepherd, Moses. The small shrine, a round enclosure 5.5 meters in diameter, was built of flat stones, many of which exhibit Nabatean inscriptions. Other inscriptions were engraved on rocks along the path leading to the mountaintop and on the rocks around the small shrine. Several kinds of priests are mentioned: *kahana,* a Semitic term for priest; and *iphkala* or *ikphala,* a Babylonian term for priest. The term *mubaqra,* possibly meaning a priest dealing with sacrifices or with temple administration, is found frequently. One person identified himself as a *kataba,* "scribe." In numerous other places in southern Sinai the term *beitiya* is mentioned, a priest in management of a temple. The only dated inscription found here is dated to 113 A.E. (219 C.E.). The publication of these inscriptions encouraged my student Uzi Avner to climb Jebel Serbal, from which other previously published[91] Nabatean inscriptions were taken. In September 1979 Avner partly excavated a small, typically Naba-

62. Sinai. Jebel Moneijah. A Nabatean inscription mentions the priest Ḥarishu, son of ʿAmayu, and his daughter ʾUmzaydu.

117

tean temple at the mountaintop. Like the larger temples in the Hauran, it consists of an inner shrine measuring 2.20 by 2.20 meters, enclosed by an outer shrine measuring 5.5 by 4.3 meters, and of a portico opening to the southwest. At a lower level is a court measuring 20.0 by 11.0 meters in which there is an altar. Both parts of the temple are connected by two flights of steps.[92] Thus, the higher mountain, Jebel Serbal, the top of which is difficult to reach, was most probably the deities' abode; the other moutain, Jebel Moneijah, was accessible to pilgrims. It is tempting to connect this region, in which the name Feiran/Paran lingers on, with earlier religious traditions.

The latest Nabatean inscriptions predate the advent of Christian monasticism into this part of the peninsula by a generation or so. This new religious movement does not seem to have a direct bearing on Nabatean history and will not be considered here. We shall now return to the Negev.

A noticeable change in the urban topography of the Negev occurred during the reigns of Diocletian and Constantine I. The citadel on the acropolis of Oboda[93] that was once considered Byzantine is quite certainly of the late third to the early fourth century.[94] The same applies to the citadel at Nessana, although the excavators were much influenced by the important discovery of the papyri at Nessana. In these documents a military unit of "the Very Loyal Theodosians" is mentioned, which resulted in dating the construction of the citadel of Nessana to the fifth century c.e.[95] The assignment of the building of the citadel of Nessana to these "Very loyal Theodosians" is taken for granted by all scholars dealing with the Negev,[96] but this is done for no good reason. Out of sixteen documents dealing with military matters at Nessana, one only mentions this military unit.[97] This document,[98] drawn and signed at Rhinocorura, quite distant from Nessana, could have reached Nessana either on the occasion of the retirement of the soldier brothers from active service at the border town of Rhinocorura or while they were on leave. All other documents just mention the "camp" ($\kappa\acute{\alpha}\sigma\tau\rho\sigma\nu$) at Nessana without naming a unit. Thus, there is no connection whatsoever between these "Theodosians" and the founding of the camp. The only

118

way to ascertain a plausible date for the construction of the citadel of Nessana is to look into the history of the city's coins. The fourth century C.E. is represented by coins of Licinius (307–24), Constantine II (317–37), Constantius II (337–61), Valens (364–78), and Valentinian II (375–92). In all probability, the citadel of Nessana was founded at the beginning of the fourth century C.E., not at the beginning of the fifth century C.E. as suggested by the excavators.[99] If this is correct, then the new great age in the history of the Negev began in the first half of the fourth century C.E. Christianity's penetration of the Negev seems to have begun in the second half of the fourth century.[100] We do not know whether this penetration met

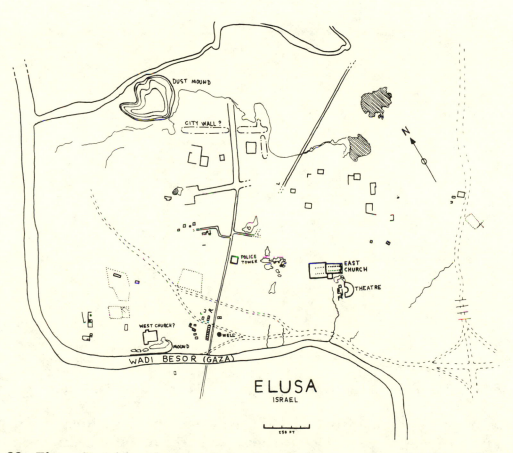

63. Elusa. Provisional plan of the site after the surveys of 1973, 1979, and 1980. (R. Fritzius).

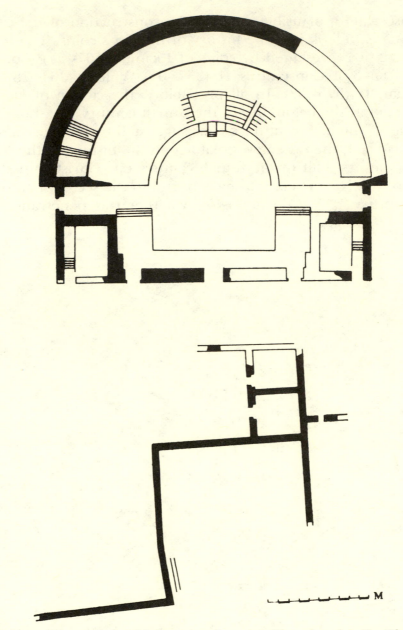

64. Elusa. Plan of the Nabatean theater. Drawing by D. Chen.

with any opposition from the old pagan communities, but at least at Elusa, capital of the district, paganism lingered on into the fifth century c.e. This is indicated by pre-Christian tombstones[101] but mainly by an official inscription found in the Nabatean theater of Elusa.[102] The inscription, which bears the name of the governor of the prov-

65. Elusa. The cavea of the Nabatean theater.

ince, Flavius Demarchus, was dedicated by the citizen Abraamius, son of Zenobius, in 349 A.E. (454/55 C.E.). Although found only forty meters away from the city cathedral, which I have dated to the fourth century, it bears no Christian symbols. After 500 C.E. this would be unthinkable.

Before turning to the urban changes that took place during this new age in the Negev, the problem of who the inhabitants of the towns of the Negev in the late Roman Byzantine period were must be considered.

The main source of evidence consists of the numerous inscriptions and papyri found at Nessana, but much evidence also comes from Oboda, Elusa, Sobata, and Ruheibah (Rehovot). In Appendix C in my PNNR, Nabatean and Arabian personal names in Greek form in the period from 350 to 650 C.E. are enumerated. This list includes 248 personal names, but the actual number of people involved was much larger, since some names were common among several people. This list should be compared with Appendix E, in

121

which biblical, Greek, Roman, and Greek-Egyptian personal names of the same period are enumerated. It includes 147 personal names, by which a larger number of persons were named because many people were named in the Negev by certain biblical names which attained great popularity.

Some of the Arabian-Nabatean names are those that have persisted from Nabatean and late Roman times, and some are new. The number of names originating in Safaitic and Thamudic is not as large as one might have expected, however. It is possible that the Arab tribesmen who penetrated the Negev from the middle of the first century C.E. onward constituted the seminomadic element that always lived in the shadow of the towns and villages and, for this reason, is little represented in the documents, which necessarily represent the urban population.

We thus find old names like Abdalgos;[103] Abdalla;[104] Abouzonainos, Azonaines;[105] Aedos, Aeidos, Alafallas, Alafallos;[106] Alfeios, Alfios;[107] Amathalla;[108] Amros;[109] Anamos, Anmos;[110] Auidos;[111] Asados;[112] Ausos[113]—and this without citing all the names that are listed under the letter A. A few of the common biblical, Greek, Roman, and Greco-Egyptian names are: Abramios,[114] Agathemeros,[115] Athanasios,[116] Alexandros,[117] Ammonios,[118] Victor,[119] Georgios,[120] and Zacharias.[121]

There is, of course, no division between groups of population having this or that type of name. Thus, Abouzonainos was the father of Abraamios,[122] and Aedos was the father of another Abraamios;[123] Alafallas was the father of Stephanos,[124] and one Alafallos was the brother of Viktor and Sergios, and another was the father of Stephanos;[125] the soldier Alobedos was the son of Sergios,[126] and the priest Alobeos was a son of Georgios, grandson of Feanes;[127] the soldier Ausos was the son of Abraamios, brother of Stephanos,[128] and the scribe Zonainos was the son of Abraamios.[129] (The frequency of the name Abraamios leads one to suspect that it became a baptismal name in the Negev.) Another Zonainos was a priest, father of Stephanos and grandfather of Ioannes. And, the other way around, persons with biblical and other non-Semitic names were related to people with Arabian-Nabatean names: Ammonios was father of Aouidos and grandfather of Thoamos;[130] Viktor was father of Alolef; another Viktor, a priest by the same name, was brother of Alafallos and Sergios; still another Viktor was son of Darebos, and a goldsmith with the name of Viktor was son of Zonai-

122

nos;[131] Dorotheos's father and son was Zonainos;[132] Elias was father of Alafallos and grandfather of Fesanes;[133] and so on.

It is not always possible to trace the Nabatean-Arabian origin of the family. Thus: "Anastasia daughter of Alexandros, wife of Patrikios son of Georgius, father superior" (on a tombstone at Nessana).[134] Iosef was the son of Arthemidoros from Nessana,[135] Benjamin Sergios, a Pharanite monk living at Sobata;[136] Viktor was the father of Sara, and another Viktor was the father of Stephanos, a priest;[137] Boethos was the father of Stephanos from Elusa, and the Boethos-Stephanos combination of names appears at Sobata;[138] Germanos was the father of Alexandros from Oboda;[139] and so on.

It would not be superfluous to cite one of the numerous documents found at Nessana in order to show how mixed (as far as onomastics is concerned) the population of a city in the Negev was. A late-seventh-century C.E. list of offerings made to the church[140] names the following people: Sergius, son of Aedos (a Nabatean name); Abraamios, son of Ammonos (could be Nabatean, Ammanu); Abraamios, son of Rokeos (doubtfully Arabian); Stephanos, son of Announes (possibly Nabatean, Haninu?); Ioannes, priest; Oualios, son of Gadimos (both Nabatean names); Sadalas, presbyter; and Georgius, son of Rokeos. There are also numerous similar documents from earlier centuries. At least two Greek documents found at Nessana do not belong to it, and no good explanation of how they came to be found at Elusa has been offered. These documents are the two daily records of the sale of dates, which must have come from the Mediterranean coast between Gaza and the borders of Egypt.[141] In the dating in these documents, instead of the Macedonian names for months, which was usual in the Negev, Egyptian names were used throughout. Some of the names are: Timotheos, son of Rufinus; Iulianus, son of Bia; Alexandros, son of Dionysos; Ioannes, son of Dionysos; Menas, son of Arsas; Anastasius, son of Hermes. One has to look carefully to find a Semitic name like Zenobius, son of Barochus, or Calonymus, son of Leuele (the first could be Jewish; the other is indeterminable). Yet, a name like Egyption leaves little doubt about its origin. A few other names also disclose the origin of the people involved. This is the case with respect to Theodoros of Samaria, or the Lybian. Lybia was a world completely different from that of Negev. It is possible that the unknown date merchants were brothers, natives of Nessana, who served many years in the border town of Rhinocorura, where they traded in dates, which abound in

123

that region, and that it is they who brought these documents back to their home, Nessana, where they were found.

This onomastic picture would not be complete without a glimpse of Appendix D, in which are listed the Nabatean-Arabian personal names in the period 650–750 C.E., that is, after the Arab conquest of the Negev. Along with remnants of the old population there are some Greek-Arabic papyri with names like: Abdeleese ben Nooman,[142] Abdella ben Alkama,[143] Abou Amer ben Abiaba,[144] Abib ben Abgar,[145] Soulaim ben Abouthamtham,[146] Abou Gaber ben Amer, Obaid ben Amer, Obaidalla ben Amer, Olae ben Amer, Said ben Amer, Soufian ben Amer, and Harim ben Amer.[147] In addition, there are names of fifty-seven Arab tribes, never heard of before in the Negev.[148] No Greek inscription in the Negev is later than 700 C.E.

Let us now turn to the changes that took place in the physical aspect of the towns of the Negev. The founding of Early Nabatean cities in the Negev influenced their future development. As we have seen, the Nabateans based their occupation of the Negev on the triangle formed by the cities of Oboda, Elusa, and Nessana, by which they dominated both the caravan trade and communication with the neighboring state of Judea. In the Hellenistic, that is, the Early Nabatean period, these towns were just large campsites; solid architecture dates only from the Middle Nabatean period. Although there is a lack of positive evidence about the way this network was organized, it would probably not be far from the truth to assume that this was a matter of public concern—at least as far as the construction of temples, the maintenance of the army, and the means of transport were concerned. Therefore, it can be argued, that the presence of relatively large numbers of inscriptions pertaining to pre-Byzantine times can be attributed to people's desire to perpetuate their name.[149] What is more important, however, and of more far-reaching consequences, is the public ground found in these cities. At Oboda and Nessana this public ground was located on an acropolis hill. At Oboda the Late Nabatean temple occupied the site of the older temple, and churches were built on the same site in the Byzantine period. At Nessana the church was built above the older Fort, which also underlies the east part of the later citadel. At Elusa matters are still not as clear as on the other sites, but the presence of a line of towers of the late Roman period and of two large churches

124

in the southern half of the town, where the Nabatean theater, and possibly also a Nabatean necropolis, are located may point to the site of the ancient acropolis.[150] In any case, the Late Nabatean town of Elusa was located in the opposite, northeastern part of the site.

In addition to these three early cities, three other cities were founded in the Middle Nabatean period: Mampsis, Sobata, and Ruheibah. Little is known about the nature of these cities in the Middle Nabatean period, but they were most probably just small road stations housing caravanseries. The introduction of agriculture infused new life into these small sites, lying in the midst of an agricultural hinterland. In this new phase in Nabatean history private enterprise must have been the basis of the new developments. At Mampsis, the town most extensively investigated, not a single Nabatean or Greco-Nabatean inscription has come to light; the only Nabatean inscription at Sobata is one of the time of Aretas IV, and a single bilingual Nabatean-Greek inscription was found at Ruheibah.[151] But it is the kind of domestic architecture on these sites that especially discloses the private nature of these sites. Owing to the lack of public authority, no new temple was built on either of these sites;[152] there were no fortifications of any kind except for towers and the solid construction of the dwellings. The only structures that must have been built as a matter of public concern were those connected with the water supply, such as damming systems near Mampsis and, with all probability, those at Sobata also.[153] In the Late Nabatan period, public concern most probably led to the construction of the large double reservoir, to the south, east, and west of which the Late Nabatean town was located.[154] The rest of the town areas of Mampsis and Sobata were divided among their occupants. The advent of Christianity caused a major problem for these towns during the later Nabatean phase in the Negev. At Sobata[155] the problem was tackled with relative ease. The cathedral, the South Church, was built to the east of the double reservoir, at the border of the old town. The only deficiencies in the planning of this building were the lack of space for a proper atrium and the somewhat irregular shape of the basilica.[156] The North Church, a monastery and pilgrimage church, was built outside the built-up area. The city then grew within these limits, and when necessity arose a third church, the Central Church, was built in the new quarter of the city.

This was fine for Sobata, a town built on rather flat terrain. It was much more complicated at Mampsis. On the south, the town,

125

with an area of ten acres, leaned on the deep ravine of Nahal Mamshit.[157] There was, of course, the large open plain to the north of the city, but since the site was surrounded by a wall in the time of Diocletian, the churches would have had to be built outside the walls, which was impossible. In order to make room for the large cathedral, the East Church, a small section of the southern city wall was dismantled; a fill was made on the steep slope; and the fifty-meter-long church was built on a rather narrow stretch of land just east of Building XII (the stable), which apparently became the bishop's dwelling, and the Building IV, the market building. The major drawback of this plan was the placement of the grand staircase to the north of the atrium instead of to its west. Townspeople who came to pray on Sunday had to use a very narrow passageway between the bell tower and the market building or walk through the streets of the market—not an ideal situation. When the contemporary smaller West Church was built, another section of the western city wall was was dismantled, and a considerable part of Building XI, possibly the house of Nilus, the man responsible for the construction of this church, was destroyed to make room for it.

The Nabatean heritage is clearly manifested in local architecture. Indeed, no houses of the size of the Mampsis dwellings were ever built, but houses were still better built and were more spacious than in other Nabatean cities.[158] The old methods of roofing by arches and flat stone slabs were still used, but softer stone was sometimes used, and the sophisticated staircase-tower was replaced by simple steps built into a wall in the court. The cutting of the stone was less carefully done. In the architecture of the East Church at Mampsis, however, Nabatean stonework may still be seen in all its former splendor. Indeed, the bell tower was already provided for by the new type of staircase, but the fifty-meter long north and south walls of the basilica and the atrium were treated in a way that only descendants of Nabatean masons could have done. Not only were the walls made of good ashlars,[159] but they were decorated by flat pilasters serving no practical purpose that were crowned by caps embellished with the old motive of a six-petal rosette, though not with Christian symbols (these symbols abound in the interior of the building).

Beginning in the late Roman period the Corinthian order was almost invariably used in the decoration of churches and synagogues in the Holy Land. The cathedral, the East Church of Elusa,

126

one of the most beautifully adorned church buildings in the Holy Land, was indeed decorated by Corinthian capitals,[160] but this was unusual. At Oboda, Nabatean capitals taken from an older Nabatean building were reused to decorate the main entrance to the South Church.[161] At Mampsis acanthus leaves were used, though differently than in the Corinthian capital; a simple abacus-type capital similar to those at Nessana[162] was consistently employed. Nothing retains the older elements as minor architectural decoration does. The use of the six-petal rosette has already been mentioned in connection with the decoration of the East Church at Mampsis. This device abounds everywhere; for example, on a lintel, together with a cross, at Nessana,[163] Sobata,[164] and Elusa.[165] It is the history of the Nabatean classical capital that is of most interest, however. Capitals of the Nabatean classical type were found at Oboda, Mampsis, Nessana, and Elusa.[166] But, although classical in form, some capitals at Mampsis have unusual features. The bosses of one pair of doorpost capitals were decorated by a human face, an ox head, and an amphora.[167] Another doorpost capital, half of which was found, probably had a smooth boss, but its face was decorated by a vine motive, and a calyculus decorated its horn. Below the horn is a palmette in low relief.[168] At Elusa there were numerous capitals of the plain classical type,[169] but the majority of the capitals, all classical in outline, had additional ornamentation. One of the simplest was a capital decorated by a rope motive, with dentils below it.[170] This motive, which is Nabatean, became very common in the Byzantine period.[171] The palmette, another very common Nabatean decorative motive, was used in a temple at Elusa both for the capitals and for the acroteria,[172] and also in the decoration of the capital of the classical Nabatean type.[173] The classical type of capital had a very long history at Elusa, at the end of which a cross decorates the boss of a capital of the classical type, together with palmettes.[174] When the Nabatean capital lost its original shape, the palmettes with a cross on the face of the capital persisted.[175] The palmette spread all over the Negev.[176] The wreath motive, a less common type of Nabatean capital, but one of far-reaching artistic influence, is found in the temple of Oboda.[177] This motive was frequently used at Oboda to decorate painted bowls.[178] It was then taken up by Nabatean goldsmiths.[179] And finally, it spread to the solid architecture of the Byzantine period.[180] These are the most easily recognizable Nabatean motives that persisted in the Byzantine period but are not the only

127

66. Elusa. A Nabatean-type capital, decorated by a cross, two birds, and two palmettes.

ones by which the continuity of Nabatean and Byzantine art in the Negev may be followed.

At the beginning of this chapter I cited the interdiction imposed on the Nabateans on drinking wine, which was an offense punishable by death. The departure of the Nabateans from their ancestral ways could not have been completed without growing grapes and producing wine. Although the chronology of the agriculture in the Negev is still a matter for future research, the beginning of viticulture in the Negev does not precede Christianity's penetration of the Negev. The grape did not figure in the Nabatean art of the Negev—or if it did, then it did covertly (e.g., if some of the small clusters that occur on a certain type of Nabatean painted bowls are grapes).[181] Bowls of this type were common in the Nabatean necropolis of Mampsis and on gold jewelry from Mampsis.[182] But at Mampsis the grape certainly did not occupy the place it did in the Nabatean art of Khirbet et-Tannur.[183] It was entirely different during the Byzantine period in the Negev. At Oboda five wine presses and two wine cellars have been found,[184] and at least three have been found at Sobata and one at Elusa.[185] Several of the Nessana

128

papyri deal with the cultivation of grapes.[186] But there is nothing that portrays the importance of wine in the life of the Negev better than the local art, as it also does at Sobata,[187] Nessana,[188] Oboda,[189] and Mampsis.[190]

The arrival in 636 c.e. of the new Islamic tribes in the Negev disturbed the delicate balance between cultivated lands and the desert. The burden of taxes the Byzantine authorities imposed on the towns of the Negev was much lighter than that imposed on towns lying north of the Beersheba Plain, which helped the towns of the Negev to survive. This changed completely after 636 c.e. Once the administration at Gaza was organized, the Muslim authorities began to impose heavy taxation on the inhabitants of Nessana (and the other towns that survived the onslaught) with demands for land taxes to be paid in gold.[191] In addition, every few months the town was forced to supply the Muslim army with wheat, oil, and money.[192] In the period between November 674 and February 677 c.e. which is amply documented, Nessana paid taxes in the form of 1,146 modii of wheat (an additional quantity of 270 modii was paid in 689 c.e.) and 1,146 sestarii of oil (and an additional 270 sestarii of oil in the same year). There was also a food tax[193] in the same period. To meet these demands Nessana paid 1,180 modii of wheat, 610 sestarii of oil, and being short of agricultural products, these were compensated for by more than 27 solidi in gold, equivalent to the price of 407 modii of wheat and 407 sestarii of oil. About 685 c.e. the following letter was sent to Nessana: "Get whatever you can collect for me since I have authority over the quota of. . . . Make sure that you do not delay an hour in bringing the poll tax and it be found sufficient for the second installment at Gaza. . . . Peace be with you!"[194] On two occasions the provincial governor felt free to demand a guide for a trip to the Holy Mount (i.e., "Mount Sinai"), a journey that could last a month, taking it for granted that the cost would be paid by the town of Nessana.[195] People and camels from Nessana were recruited for compulsory service in such distant places as Caesarea and Scythopolis.[196] It is no wonder that one of the end of the seventh century c.e. documents reads: "We wish to inform your Noble Magnificence, Beloved of God, that we have received a letter from His Magnificence, Lord Samuel, that he personally invites both of you and us at one and the same time to appeal to our most esteemed Governor to grant us relief [?]. For they caused us and you serious distress and are unable to bear the burden of such taxation. Note, therefore, that tomorrow, Monday, we shall be in Gaza. There are twenty of us. Will you too please come [?] immediately so that all of us may be of one mind and of one accord [?] After you have read the present letter, send it to Nessana. We wrote to Sobata. Good luck and good health to you!"[197]

It has been overlooked that in all these demands for products of the land, one product, the most important for the economy of the Negev, was not mentioned: wine. Although any definite proof is lacking, it is nevertheless likely that the new fanatic Muslim authorities either forbade the production of wine altogether or simply cut the producer off from the wine market. It is no wonder that, like other parts of the Holy Land, the Negev returned to its starting point, becoming desert again, completing the cycle of 1,500 years of Nabatean history.

Notes

CHAPTER ONE

1. On Nabatean chronology see Negev, 1966, pp. 89–98; Negev, 1969b, pp. 5–14; Negev, 1967a, pp. 46–55; Negev, 1976a, pp. 125–133.
2. Dalman, 1908, p. 44.
3. F. M. Abel, "L'expédition des grecs a Pétra en 312 avant J. C.," *RB* 35 (1921): 376–391.
4. Hornblower, 1981, pp. 144–153.
5. Diodorus, *Bibliotheca* XIX.94.4–5. All translations cited here are those of R. M. Geer (Loeb Classical Library, 1950–1957).
6. Negev, 1967b, pp. 250–255; Negev, 1977a, pp. 250–255; Negev, 1977b, pp. 66–71. During all these years I have been working on a corpus of Nabatean personal names (PNNR). The corpus comprises two main parts: (a) a survey of personal names found in the whole Nabatean realm, and (b) personal names found in the Negev. In the first part the Nabatean realm is subdivided into four major regions: (1) northern Arabia (NA); (2) Sinai, Egypt, and the Negev (SEN); (3) Edom and Moab (EM); and (4) the Hauran (H). The number of occurrences is given with each personal name; references to the literature with respect to personal names that were recorded after the compilation of *CIS* II, the publication of *RES,* and the index in Cantineau II. The following eight columns in the corpus consist of comparisons with personal names in other Arabian languages: Lihyanite, Safaitic, Thamudic, Himyarite, Minaean, Qatabanian, Sabaean, and Palmyrene. The number of occurrences is given in each case. The last part of the corpus leaves space for notes, translations of the names into Arabic and other Semitic languages, the Greek form of Nabatean personal names, and so forth. This general list is followed by numerous analytical tables (pp. XCVI–CLI) that enumerate personal names occurring only in NA (pp. XCVI–XCVIII), only in SEN (pp. XCIX–CI), only in EM (pp. CII–CIII), and only in the H (p. CIV). These, in turn, are followed by tables in which are enumerated personal names occurring in all four regions (p. CV), in three regions (p. CVI), and in two regions (pp. CVII–CVIII), including all possible combinations of regions. These are followed by tables arranged according to the possible meaning or meanings of the personal name, always in connection with the geographical divisions explained above. Thus are enumerated names with theophoric and allied meanings (pp. CIX–CXI), geographical names (p. CXI), tribal and

131

ethnic names (p. CXI), Greek and Roman names (p. CXII), occupational names (p. CXIII), and names relating to celestial and other heavenly bodies (p. CXIII), to animals, reptiles, etc. (p. CXIV), to plants, agriculture, etc. (p. CXIV), to physical qualities (p. CV), and to spiritual qualities, positive and negative (p. CV). The last series of tables in this part provides the possible affiliation of Nabatean personal names with other groups of Semitic languages: Nabatean personal names unparalleled in other Arabian languages (pp. CXVIII–CXX); names of possibly Nabatean origin, on the assumption that their occurrence in Nabatean inscriptions outnumbers their occurrence in other Arabian languages (pp. CXXI–CXXIII); names of possibly northern or southern Arabian origin (pp. CXXIV–CXXXIX); Palmyrene personal names and their relation to Nabatean and other Arabian names (pp. CXL–CXLII); and personal names of possibly common Semitic origin (pp. CXLIII–CLI). The second part of the study includes five appendixes: A. Nabatean-Arabian names in the Negev 200 B.C.E.–300 C.E. (nos. 2000–2031); B. Nabatean-Arabian names in Greek form c. 200–350 C.E. (nos. 2032–2057); C. Nabatean and Arabian names in Greek form 350–650 C.E. (nos. 2058–2306); D. Nabatean-Arabian names in Greek form 650–750 C.E. (nos. 2500–2644); and E. Biblical, Greek, Roman, and Greco-Egyptian names (nos. 3000–3145). Finally, special attention is given to the name Flavius (no. 3146) and to the name Abraamius, which is very common in the Negev. The origin of each name is stated in all cases, whether from this or that town in the Negev. I am now working on the detailed preface of the corpus.

7. For a résumé of the different evaluations of these rock inscriptions see Cantineau I, pp. 22–25.

8. On PNNR, see note 6, above. In various of my publications different numbers are given. These reflect different stages in the research.

9. See, e.g., Stark, 1971, p. 144.

10. Winnett and Reed, 1970; see index 4 of the Thamudic inscriptions, p. 194.

11. Negev, 1967b, pp. 250–255.

12. See Negev, 1977c, p. 538.

13. PNNR, nos. 415–416.

14. PNNR, no. 397.

15. PNNR, no. 951.

16. PNNR, no. 182; *ICPAN*, p. 119; Cantineau II, p. 72.

17. PNNR, no. 288; *ICPAN*, p. 166; Cantineau II, p. 78.

18. PNNR, no. 836; *ICPAN*, p. 402; Cantineau II, p. 127; Wuthnow, pp. 86, 154.

19. PNNR, no. 845; *ICPAN*, p. 410; Cantineau II, p. 127.

20. PNNR, no. 885; *ICPAN*, p. 429; Cantineau II, p. 130.

21. PNNR, no. 1033; *ICPAN*, pp. 467, 489; Cantineau II, p. 143.

22. PNNR, no. 891; Cantineau II, p. 130.

23. PNNR, no. 939; *ICPAN*, no. 414; Cantineau II, p. 134; Stark, pp. 45, 107; Wuthnow, pp. 25, 160.

24. PNNR, no. 1192; *ICPAN*, p. 347; Cantineau II, p. 154; Wuthnow, pp. 105, 174.

25. Jaussen-Savignac, *Mission* I, nos. 334, 335.

26. Negev, 1976b, pp. 223–231.

27. Negev, 1976b, p. 214.

28. Ibid.

29. PNNR, no. 132; *Nessana* I, p. 203.

30. PNNR, no. 391; Littman and Meredith, 1953, pp. 1–27; 1954, pp. 211–246.

31. Littman and Meredith, 1954, p. 225.

32. PNNR, no. 768; Cantineau II, p. 123.

33. PNNR, no. 778; Cantineau II, p. 124.

34. PNNR, no. 981; Cantineau II, p. 137.

35. PNNR, no. 80; Cantineau II, p. 61.

36. PNNR, table on p. CXIII.

37. Negev, 1976b, passim.

38. PNNR, no. 346; *ICPAN*, pp. 648–649; Cantineau II, p. 90.

39. PNNR, no. 465; *ICPAN*, p. 202; Cantineau II, p. 97.

40. PNNR, no. 580; *ICPAN*, p. 648; Cantineau II, p. 104.

41. PNNR, no. 871; *ICPAN*, p. 455; Cantineau II, p. 129.

42. PNNR, no. 1058; *ICPAN*, p. 275; Cantineau II, p. 146.

43. PNNR, no. 1075; *ICPAN*, p. 288.
44. PNNR, no. 1106; *ICPAN*, p. 341; Cantineau II, p. 149.
45. PNNR, no. 1186; *ICPAN*, p. 353; Cantineau II, p. 153.
46. PNNR, nos. 16, 17, 18, 1027; *ICPAN*, p. 118.
47. PNNR, no. 347; *ICPAN*, pp. 648–649; Cantineau II, p. 90.
48. PNNR, nos. 65, 67; *ICPAN*, p. 184; Cantineau II, p. 60.
49. PNNR, nos. 376, 377; *ICPAN*, p. 295; Cantineau II, p. 91.
50. PNNR, nos. 442, 491; *ICPAN*, p. 197.
51. PNNR, nos. 754, 757; *ICPAN*, p. 586; Cantineau II, p. 122.
52. PNNR, nos. 1158, 1159; *ICPAN*, p. 357; Cantineau II, p. 152.
53. PNNR, no. 762; *ICPAN*, p. 580; Cantineau II, p. 123.
54. PNNR, no. 751; *ICPAN*, p. 598; Cantineau II, p. 122.
55. PNNR, no. 907; *ICPAN*, p. 440; Cantineau II, p. 132.
56. PNNR, no. 872; *ICPAN*, p. 455; Cantineau II, p. 129.
57. PNNR, no. 1030; Cantineau II, p. 143.
58. PNNR, no. 1042; Cantineau II, p. 144.
59. PNNR, nos. 48, 49, 50; *ICPAN*, p. 111.
60. PNNR, nos. 248, 249, 255.
61. PNNR, no. 382.
62. PNNR, no. 87.
63. PNNR, no. 1107.
64. PNNR, no. 1213.
65. PNNR, no. 188; see also *ICPAN*, pp. 111, 527.
66. On the diety 'Allah or 'Illah see Starcky, *Dictionnaire*, cols. 985–986.
67. PNNR, nos. 50, 51; *ICPAN*, p. 63.
68. Wuthnow, pp. 30, 125.
69. PNNR, no. 52.
70. PNNR, no. 107.
71. PNNR, nos. 247, 248; *ICPAN*, p. 158.
72. Wuthnow, pp. 39, 134.
73. PNNR, no. 402.
74. PNNR, no. 467.
75. *ICPAN*, p. 205.
76. Wuthnow, pp. 23, 142.
77. PNNR, nos. 670, 674.
78. See Cantineau II, p. 117.
79. PNNR, no. 780.
80. PNNR, no. 1108; see also *ICPAN*, p. 320.
81. PNNR, no. 1129; see also Cantineau II, p. 150.
82. PNNR, nos. 1144, 1147.
83. Cantineau II, 151.
84. PNNR, no. 68; Cantineau II, p. 60.
85. PNNR, no. 1233.
86. PNNR, no. 7.
87. See *ICPAN*, p. 17.
88. PNNR, no. 102.
89. See *ICPAN*, p. 75.
90. PNNR, no. 309; *ICPAN*, p. 626; Cantineau II, p. 87.
91. Wuthnow, pp. 21, 136.
92. PNNR, no. 399.
93. PNNR, no. 454; *ICPAN*, p. 227.
94. Wuthnow, pp. 16, 141.
95. PNNR, no. 1028.
96. PNNR, no. 1098.
97. *ICPAN*, p. 309.
98. Cantineau II, p. 148.
99. PNNR, no. 1126.
100. Cantineau II, p. 150.
101. PNNR, no. 1133.
102. Cantineau II, p. 63.
103. PNNR, no. 337.
104. See *ICPAN*, p. 651.
105. Wuthnow, pp. 91, 136.
106. PNNR, no. 1070.
107. PNNR, no. 1174.
108. PNNR, no. 51.
109. PNNR, no. 793.
110. PNNR, no. 1214.
111. Wuthnow, pp. 53, 54, 175.
112. PNNR, no. 451.
113. On this god see Starcky, *Histoire*, pp. 203–206.
114. PNNR, no. 282.
115. *ICPAN*, p. 214.
116. Cantineau II, p. 84.
117. PNNR, no. 329.
118. *ICPAN*, p. 637.
119. Wuthnow, pp. 91, 136.
120. PNNR, no. 354.
121. *ICPAN*, p. 647.
122. PNNR, no. 631.
123. *ICPAN*, p. 537.
124. PNNR, no. 865.
125. *ICPAN*, p. 418.
126. PNNR, no. 890.
127. *ICPAN*, p. 418.
128. PNNR, no. 1052.
129. *ICPAN*, p. 567.

130. PNNR, no. 101.
131. *ICPAN*, p. 75; Cantineau II, p. 64.
132. Wuthnow, pp. 20, 129.
133. PNNR, no. 246.
134. *ICPAN*, p. 63.
135. Wuthnow, pp. 39, 134.
136. PNNR, no. 430.
137. *ICPAN*, p. 209.
138. PNNR, no. 786.
139. *ICPAN*, p. 397.
140. Wuthnow, pp. 8, 153.
141. PNNR, no. 866.
142. *ICPAN*, p. 418.
143. PNNR, no. 914.
144. *ICPAN*, p. 437.
145. PNNR, no. 964.
146. *ICPAN*, p. 471.
147. PNNR, no. 1044.
148. *ICPAN*, pp. 482, 483.
149. PNNR, no. 423.
150. *ICPAN*, p. 208.
151. PNNR, no. 725; see *ICPAN*, p. 591.
152. PNNR, no. 469; see *ICPAN*, p. 205.
153. Wuthnow, pp. 23, 142.
154. PNNR, no. 502; Cantineau II, p. 101.
155. *ICPAN*, p. 388.
156. PNNR, no. 726.
157. PNNR, no. 1002.
158. *ICPAN*, p. 372.
159. PNNR, no. 1125; *ICPAN*, p. 349; Cantineau II, p. 149.
160. PNNR, no. 1132; *ICPAN*, p. 354; Cantineau II, p. 150.
161. PNNR, nos. 1132–1133.
162. Wuthnow, pp. 106, 170.
163. PNNR, no. 1049.
164. *ICPAN*, p. 263.
165. Stark, 1971, pp. 49, 111.
166. Wuthnow, pp. 96, 166.
167. PNNR, no. 824.
168. PNNR, no. 1073.
169. *ICPAN*, p. 286.
170. Stark, 1971, pp. 49, 112.
171. Cantineau II, pp. 169–170.
172. PNNR, no. 797.
173. PNNR, no. 1217.
174. Wuthnow, pp. 54, 175.
175. PNNR, no. 1216.
176. *ICPAN*, p. 141.
177. Stark, 1971, pp. 55, 117.
178. Wuthnow, pp. 54, 175.

179. PNNR, no. 1235.
180. *ICPAN*, p. 137.
181. PNNR, no. 993.
182. *ICPAN*, p. 338; see Cantineau II, p. 139.
183. PNNR, no. 643.
184. *ICPAN*, p. 565.
185. PNNR, no. 1149.
186. Wuthnow, pp. 103, 171.
187. *ICPAN*, p. 326.
188. PNNR, no. 1187; Cantineau II, p. 153.
189. *ICPAN*, p. 353.
190. PNNR, no. 325; Cantineau II, pp. 88, 160.
191. *ICPAN*, p. 632.
192. PNNR, no. 338.
193. Stark, 1971, pp. 15, 85.
194. *ICPAN*, p. 652.
195. Wuthnow, pp. 91, 136.
196. Cantineau II, p. 169.
197. PNNR, no. 341.
198. PNNR, no. 386; Winnett and Reed, 1970, no. 24, p. 146.
199. PNNR, no. 809; Cantineau II, p. 116.
200. *ICPAN*, p. 400.
201. PNNR, no. 810.
202. PNNR, no. 1221; Cantineau II, p. 116.
203. See Cantineau II, pp. 128, 169.
204. PNNR, no. 795; Cantineau II, p. 128.
205. See Cantineau II, pp. 128, 170.
206. PNNR, no. 789; Cantineau II, p. 76.
207. PNNR, no. 106; Cantineau II, p. 26.
208. PNNR, no. 788; Cantineau II, p. 76.
209. Wuthnow, pp. 7, 154; *Nessana* I, index, p. 333.
210. See Cantineau II, pp. 142, 170.
211. PNNR, no. 388; Cantineau II, pp. 92, 142.
212. Wuthnow, pp. 49, 138.
213. PNNR, no. 281; Cantineau II, p. 142.
214. PNNR, no. 822.
215. See Cantineau II, pp. 65, 170.
216. PNNR, no. 105; Yadin, 1962, p. 239.
217. PNNR, no. 153; Cantineau II, p. 68.
218. PNNR, no. 785; Cantineau II, pp. 65, 170.
219. See Cantineau II, pp. 76, 170.
220. PNNR, no. 212; Cantineau II, p. 76.
221. PNNR, no. 213; Cantineau II, p. 76.
222. PNNR, no. 211; Cantineau II, pp. 76, 170.

223. Wuthnow, pp. 38, 133.
224. *ICPAN*, pp. 154–155.
225. Stark, 1971, pp. 13, 81.
226. See Cantineau II, pp. 104, 170.
227. PNNR, no. 100; Cantineau II, p. 104.
228. See Cantineau II, pp. 112, 170.
229. PNNR, no. 1219; *ICPAN*, p. 658; Cantineau II, p. 105.
230. See Cantineau II, pp. 112, 170.
231. PNNR, no. 807; Cantineau II, p. 112.
232. PNNR, no. 1053; Cantineau II, pp. 112, 145.
233. See Cantineau II, pp. 116, 170.
234. PNNR, no. 812; Cantineau II, p. 116; *ICPAN*, p. 567.
235. See Cantineau II, pp. 142, 170.
236. PNNR, no. 1035; Cantineau II, p. 142.
237. Wuthnow, pp. 65, 164.
238. PNNR, no. 1013; Cantineau II, p. 142, and see *ICPAN*, p. 412.
239. Wuthnow, pp. 65, 164.
240. PNNR, no. 1215; see Milik and Starcky, 1975, p. 118.
241. PNNR, no. 586; Cantineau II, p. 108.
242. *ICPAN*, p. 495.
243. PNNR, no. 553; Cantineau II, p. 106.
244. *ICPAN*, p. 506.
245. PNNR, nos. 602, 603; Cantineau II, pp. 73–74.
246. Wuthnow, p. 18.
247. PNNR, no. 569; Cantineau II, p. 107.
248. *ICPAN*, p. 505.
249. Stark, 1971, pp. 29, 92.
250. Wuthnow, pp. 64, 65, 146.
251. PNNR, no. 177; Cantineau II, p. 70.
252. *ICPAN*, p. 94.
253. PNNR, no. 414; Cantineau II, pp. 94–95.
254. *ICPAN*, p. 177.
255. Stark, 1971, pp. 20, 87.
256. Cantineau II, p. 94.
257. Negev, 1969b, pp. 5–14.
258. Starcky, *Dictionnaire*, col. 928.
259. Unpublished.
260. Unpublished.
261. Negev, 1976c, pp. 89–95.
262. Unpublished.
263. Negev, 1974b, pp. 9–13.
264. Tushingham, *Dibon*, pp. 50–51.
265. Parr, Sequence, pp. 348–381.
266. Negev-Sivan, 1977, pp. 109–131.
267. Negev, 1976a, p. 125, notes 3, 4, 5.
268. Negev, 1976b, pp. 203–236.
269. Negev, 1976b, pp. 223–231.
270. Winnet and Reed, 1970, pp. 108–137.
271. Negev, 1969b, pp. 89–98.
272. Negev, 1982a, pp. 119–127.
273. For references to classical literature see Negev, 1982, pp. 125–126.
274. See *Geog*. XVI.2.24.
275. Negev, 1961, pp. 113–118.

CHAPTER TWO

1. Parr, Sequence, p. 370.
2. Horsfield, 1942, e.g., no. 34, p. 119 (a Megarian bowl); no. 36, p. 120 (a red-glazed bowl); no. 41, p. 122 (a stamped jar handle); nos. 83–86, p. 129 (eastern sigillata bowls); nos. 91–106, pp. 133–134 (Rodian stamped jar handles); etc.
3. Grace, *Nessana* I, pp. 106–130.
4. Negev, 1985.
5. Negev, 1977c, pl. I, upper left (a Megarian bowl).
6. On these matters see Negev, 1977c, pp. 562–563.
7. See e.g., Doe, *South Arabia*, pls. 27–35; some of the vessels are tentatively dated to the first to second centuries C.E.; figs. 11–13 on pp. 138–141.
8. Negev, 1974b, passim.
9. Kendall, *Nessana* I, pp. 29–30.
10. *Nessana* I, pl. LXVIII.
11. *Nessana* I, pp. 270–303, pls. XLIII–LXI.
12. *Nessana* I, p. 270.
13. *Nessana* I, p. 285.
14. *Nessana* I, p. 302.
15. Unpublished.
16. Personal discussion with the author.
17. Parr, Sequence, passim.
18. Ibid.; the phases are dated by coins to the period between Aretas II and Aretas IV, i.e., between 97 B.C.E. and 9 B.C.E.–40 C.E. However, coins of Aretas II are very difficult to distinguish from those of Aretas III (85–62 B.C.E.); see also Meshorer, *Coins*, pp. 9–16.
19. The phase is dated to Aretas IV.
20. The phase is dated to Aretas IV and possibly to Rabel II.
21. Jaussen-Savignac, *Mission* I, p. 146

135

(sculptors); p. 149 (sculptor); p. 155 (sculptors); p. 157 (sculptor); and numerous other sculptors are mentioned in other inscriptions, all with Nabatean personal names. Other artisans used the verb "to make."

22. Savignac, 1933, pp. 413–417. The artisans who worked on the construction of the temple, all of whom had Nabatean personal names, identify themselves either as builders (*bania* in Nabatean) or as artists *(amanah)*. The entire temple is painted, and it may have been the painters who termed themselves artists.

23. See Cantineau II, p. 64.

24. *RES*, 1088, 2: Wahab 'allahi the plasterer. See Cantineau II, p. 149.

25. Browning, *Petra*, p. 48.

26. Ibid., pp. 49–51.

27. Horsfield, 1938, pls. XLVIII–L and pp. 20–25. See these pages for the description of several other rock-cut houses.

28. Murray and Ellis, passim.

29. Ibid., pl. VI.

30. Ibid., p. 29.

31. Of these, only two were investigated: Qasr Bint Fara'un, discovered many years ago, and a temple excavated more recently by Hammond (see Hammond, 1977/78, pp. 81–107).

32. Jaussen-Savignac, *Mission* I, pp. 405–409.

33. Savignac-Horsfield, 1935, pp. 245–247.

34. Glueck, *DD,* passim.

35. Butler, *PPAES,* pp. 365–402.

36. Unpublished.

37. Negev-Sivan, 1977, pp. 109–131.

38. Negev, 1980, pp. 5–32; Negev, 1983, pp. 97–126.

39. Yadin, 1965, pp. 37–49, pl. 5.

40. These sites were excavated by R. Cohen on behalf of the Israeli Department of Antiquities and Museums. No reports have yet been published.

41. On bibliography for, and discussion of, these matters see Negev, 1982a.

42. For a translation of this inscription see Cantineau II, p. 5.

43. See Evenari, *Negev,* passim.

44. Butler, *PPAES,* pp. 11–17.

45. Ibid.

46. Hebrew edition of note 43 above (Jerusalem, 1980), p. 37.

47. Negev, 1980, fig. 1.11, showing the east wall of Building I.

48. Ibid., fig. 1.12.

49. Negev, 1973, pp. 364–383.

50. Woolley and Lawrence, pp. 123–124, fig. 55.

51. Negev, 1976c, pp. 89–95.

52. Negev, 1981c, pp. 589–591, pls. XXII–XXIV.

53. Negev, 1981a, no. 13, pp. 26–27.

54. See photographs and reconstruction in Negev, 1983, pp. 108–109; Negev, 1980, fig. 1.4B.

55. Browning, *Petra,* p. 49.

56. Butler, *PPAES,* I11.88, p. 111; I11.95, p. 120; I11.96, p. 122; I11.126, p. 142, and illustrations of numerous other stables.

57. On the capitals see Negev, 1974a, pp. 153–159.

58. Negev, 1983, p. 117.

59. Ibid., p. 110.

60. Negev, 1963, pp. 117–122.

61. Negev, 1981a, pp. 11–27.

CHAPTER THREE

1. Kammerer, *Petra,* p. 371.

2. Starcky, *Dictionnaire,* col. 1016.

3. Wright, 1969, pp. 113–116.

4. Meyers, *Ossuaries,* passim.

5. *B-D* I.

6. *B-D* I, tomb no. 4, fig. 222, p. 196 (loculi on two walls); no. 6, fig. 224, p. 197; no. 32, fig. 234, p. 255 (empty burial chamber); no. 244, fig. 306, p. 275 (the "Roman Tomb," empty chamber); no. 351, fig. 325, p. 295 (one loculus); no. 624, fig. 391, p. 361 (no loculi); no. 633, fig. 393, p. 363 (Turqmaniye Tomb, no loculi). The following monuments are among the so-called Royal Tombs: no. 661, fig. 406, p. 371 (a small burial chamber with numerous loculi in three walls); no. 676, fig. 410, p. 374 (numerous large loculi in two walls); no. 763, fig. 428, p. 382 (the tomb of Sextius Florentinus, loculi in two walls); no. 770, fig. 440, p. 391 (three burial chambers with no loculi); no. 771, fig. 443, p. 393 (loculi in three walls).

7. Horsfield, 1939, p. 104, fig. 9.

8. Horsfield, 1939, pp. 104–105.

9. Jaussen-Savignac, *Mission* II, p. 89, fig. 3.

10. Jaussen-Savignac, *Mission* I, fig. 157 on p. 342.

11. Jaussen-Savignac, *Mission* I, pp. 359–363, figs. 174–176.

12. Jaussen-Savignac, *Mission* I, fig. 178, pp. 363–366.

13. Jaussen-Savignac, *Mission* I, fig. 188, p. 376.

14. Jaussen-Savignac, *Mission* I, pp. 378–382.

15. Jaussen-Savignac, *Mission* II, p. 80, fig. 24, pl. XXXVIII, 3.

16. Negev, 1976b, pp. 209, 216; see Jaussen-Savignac, *Mission* I, pp. 162–163.

17. Negev, 1971, pp. 120–124.

18. Negev-Sivan, 1977, pp. 118–119, fig. 12, 79.

19. Negev-Sivan, 1977, fig. 7.

20. Negev, 1971, p. 121, pl. 23A, Tombs 109 and 110. These boxes were discovered outside, southeast of the perimeter of the necropolis, and are not on the plan shown in fig. 1.

21. Negev, 1971, pp. 21–22, fig. 5, pl. 24C-D.

22. Unpublished.

23. Negev, 1971. Tombs 123 and 125, excavated after the completion of the report on the excavations of the necropolis, were not included.

24. Negev, 1971, pp. 124–125, pl. 25A-B.

25. Glueck, *DD,* plans A, H; see also the chapter entitled "Dining with Divinity," pp. 163 ff.

26. Negev, 1877c, pp. 613–619.

27. Butler, *PPAES,* pp. 365–399.

28. Bachmann, *Petra,* fig. 50, p. 58.

29. *B-D* I, no. 4, figs. 222–223, pp. 395–397; no. 766, fig. 434, pp. 398–399.

30. Bachmann, *Petra,* fig. 66, p. 76.

31. *B-D* I, no. 772, fig. 445, p. 395.

32. *B-D* I, no. 765, fig. 431, p. 385.

33. *B-D* I, no. 633, figs. 397, 400, pp. 364–366.

34. Cantineau II, pp. 3–5.

35. Dalman, 1908, passim; Dalman, *NPF,* passim.

36. Jaussen-Savignac, *Mission* I, pp. 409–430, figs. 200–226.

37. Negev, 1971, pp. 111–114, figs. 1–4, pl. 21C.

38. Negev, 1971, fig. 1, pl. 21C.

39. Negev-Sivan, 1977, pp. 113–115, fig. 5, 31–38.

40. Negev-Sivan, 1977, p. 119.

41. Negev-Sivan, 1977, pp. 111–113, 118–119, figs. 1–4.

42. Negev-Sivan, 1977, pp. 115–116, figs. 1, 6–7.

43. Negev-Sivan, 1977, pp. 117–119, figs. 1, 11–12.

44. Unpublished.

45. Horsfield, 1942, passim.

46. Woolley and Lawrence, p. 109.

47. Horsfield, 1942, pp. 151–152.

48. Murray and Ellis, pl. XIV.

49. On the jewelry see Negev, 1983, pp. 140–141; Negev, 1971, pl. 26.

50. Rosenthal, 1970, pp. 34–38, pls. 17–18. Dr. Rosenthal-Heginbottom was responsible for the excavation of almost all the interiors of the tombs in the Nabatean necropolis at Mampsis during the years 1965 to 1967, and it is in great part due to her diligence that nothing is missing from this treasure.

51. Patrich, 1983, pp. 86–88.

52. Negev, 1969a, pp. 89–106; Negev, 1978, pp. 110–112, 236–239, 274–276.

53. Glueck, *DD,* pls. 46, 48, pp. 395 ff.

CHAPTER FOUR

1. See *EB* 6, col. 356.

2. Kammerer, *Petra,* pp. 396–397.

3. Ibid., p. 417.

4. Starcky, *Dictionnaire,* cols. 990–992.

5. See *EB* 6, cols. 144–149.

6. This statement was very often taken too seriously by scholars. It was only natural for Strabo to defend Aelius Gallus's lack of experience (if not much more than that) in preparing the Roman army for a desert campaign by building ships instead of using the well-trodden caravan routes leading from Egypt (or from Judea, which was a friendly country) over Sinai to Aila and from there to Egra, which he visited anyway. It is true that the Arabians had no experience in naval combat, but even though they were

mainly "hucksters," they succeeded in protecting their caravan trade for about seventy-five years following the Roman failure.

7. This perhaps explains the fact that Nabatean kings ran their kingdom for 30 (Malichus I), 21 (Obodas II), 49 (Aretas IV), 30 (Malichus II), and 36 (Rabel II) long years!

8. See the translator's (Thackeray) note m, p. 109.

9. In this battle Herod was severely beaten by the Nabateans.

10. Steph. Byz., index, p. 729.

11. Steph. Byz., index, p. 736.

12. Doe, *South Arabia*, p. 19.

13. For general plans of Oboda see Kammerer, *Petra*, atlas, pl. 137,1; Woolley and Lawrence, fig. 24 on p. 94; Wiegand, *Sinai*, fig. 82 on p. 84.

14. These are clearly seen on the plan of Oboda in Wiegand, *Sinai*.

15. *Nessana* I, pl. LXII.

16. Euting, 1891, pl. 23, both engraved by a man named ᶜAbd-'allahi son of 'Aᶜala.

17. See Negev, 1983, p. 101, for drawing and date.

18. Horsfield, 1942, no. 52, pl. XII; no. 250, pl. XXX; no. 449, pl. XLVI.

19. Report in preparation.

20. Negev, 1961, pp. 133–138; Negev, 1963, pp. 113–117.

21. Negev, 1963, pp. 113–117.

22. Naveh, 1970, pp. 371–374.

23. Eissfeldt, 1969, pp. 217–227.

24. See Negev, 1961, p. 136, for references.

25. Negev, 1963, pp. 117–124.

26. This inscription was discovered by Mr. Roones of the Sedeh Boker branch of the Ben Gurion University of the Negev. It is engraved on a flat, very large smooth pebble buried in the midst of ancient fields. I made an attempt to decipher the inscription but soon ran into difficulties. I then called for help from my colleague, Professor J. Naveh, who completed the reading of the inscription, but he too had difficulty translating the fourth and fifth lines, which, although written in Nabatean script, were in Arabic. It was then that Professor G. Shaked was called in to contribute his knowledge of old Arabic. See the forthcoming article "Obodas the God" *IEJ*, in preparation.

27. Cantineau II, p. 6.

28. Cantineau II, p. 7.

29. Negev, 1961, pp. 135–137; Negev, 1963, pp. 113–114.

30. Cantineau II, pp. 49–50.

31. Negev, 1961, pp. 127–128, pl. 28b.

32. Negev, 1961, pl. 29b-c.

33. Negev, 1961, pp. 128–129, pl. 29a.

34. Negev, 1961, p. 131, pl. 30a.

35. Negev, 1981a, pl. 1.31; Negev, 1983, pp. 64, 65, 89.

36. Negev, 1981a, p. 12, nos. 1a, 1b.

37. Negev, 1981a, p. 13, no. 1c.

38. Negev, 1981a, p. 13, no. 1d.

39. Negev, 1981a, p. 13, no. 1e.

40. Negev, 1981a, p. 14, no. 1f.

41. Negev, 1981a, pp. 14–15, no. 2.

42. Negev, 1981a, pp. 15–18, no. 3.

43. Negev, 1981a, pp. 18–19, no. 4.

44. Negev, 1981a, pp. 20–23, no. 7.

45. Negev, 1981a, pp. 26–27, no. 13.

46. PNNR, no. 394.

47. PNNR, nos. 1168, 1169, 1170, 1172. The form of the inscription is common to all four regions.

48. PNNR, no. 748.

49. Josephus, *Jewish Antiquities* XVI.284.

50. PNNR, no. 52.

51. PNNR, nos. 1071, 1079.

52. PNNR, nos. 788, 789, 790.

53. PNNR, no. 817.

54. PNNR, no. 323.

55. PNNR, no. 1170.

56. PNNR, no. 908.

57. PNNR, no. 583.

58. PNNR, no. 253.

59. PNNR, no. 1037.

60. PNNR, no. 667.

61. PNNR, no. 56.

62. PNNR, no. 785.

63. PNNR, no. 903.

64. PNNR, no. 1146.

65. PNNR, no. 213.

66. Negev, 1981a, no. 6, p. 19.

67. Negev, 1981a, no. 3, pp. 15–16; no. 4, p. 18; no. 12, pp. 26–27.

68. Negev, 1981a, commentary to inscription no. 3, p. 16.
69. Ibid., note 17.
70. Starcky, *Dictionnaire,* col. 1002.
71. Negev, 1981a, no. 8, pp. 23–24.
72. Woolley and Lawrence, fig. 24 on p. 94.
73. Negev, 1973, p. 273, pls. III, IVb.
74. Negev, 1981a, p. 27.
75. See Bellinger in *Nessani* I, pp. 70–71.
76. Negev, 1981d, pp. 17–18.
77. Hornblower, 1981, p. 27.
78. Identified generally with Ras Muhammad at the southern tip of Sinai.
79. Translation of C. H. Oldfather, *Diodorus of Sicily,* vol. II (Loeb Classical Library, 1961), pp. 209–213.
80. See Rosenthal in Negev, 1977, pp. 95–100.
81. Negev, 1967b, pp. 250–255; Negev, 1981b, pp. 66–71.
82. Cantineau I, pp. 22–25.
83. Cantineau I, p. 25.
84. Euting, 1891, pp. x–xi; Cantineau I, p. 24.
85. The relation of Nabatean to Greco-Nabatean inscriptions has never been investigated. Following are some examples that I collected from the plates in Euting, 1891. Thus, pl. 14, nos. 252–253; pl. 19, no. 342, has a Nabatean name in Greek. The cross at the side of the inscription does not necessarily belong to it; pl. 22, no. 486, has a Nabatean name in Greek, written in reverse (from right to left); pl. 35, no. 596, has the longest bilingual inscription. More inscriptions of this kind may be found in *CIS* II.1.2.
86. See Negev, 1977a, map of ancient Sinai and inscription no. 17, p. 14 (the names of the writer and his father and grandfather, who visited seven different localities); no. 208, p. 54 (two brothers and the name of their father, who visited two sites, among which was the temple at Jebel Serbal); no. 212, p. 54 (the writer and name of his father, who visited two sites, one of which was the mining area of Wadi Mughara); no. 218, pp. 55–56 (three brothers and their father; the same family, either all brothers together, or in groups of two, or separately, are mentioned in fourteen different localities); and numerous other similar inscriptions.
87. Ibid., no. 210, p. 54; no. 220, p. 56; no. 224, p. 57; and numerous other inscriptions.
88. Moritz, 1916, pp. 27 ff.
89. On this matter see also Naveh, 1970.
90. Negev, 1977b; see also Negev, 1980a, for a detailed description of the site.
91. Negev, 1971a, pp. 183–184.
92. This important find was only summarily published in *Hadashot Archeologiot* (Archaeological News) of the Israeli Department of Antiquities and Museums, April 1981, p. 39 (Hebrew).
93. See Negev, 1980, aerial photograph, fig. 1.8, p. 10, and plan 1.9, p. 13.
94. Negev, 1977d, p. 28. The large Nabatean military camp was partly dismantled and its stones were taken for the construction of the new, smaller citadel. The inner walls of the camp were built of large stones, whereas smaller stones, taken from Late Nabatean houses (a Nabatean inscription of 126 C.E. was built into the east wall of the citadel), were used for the construction of the outer walls. In the course of the excavations made in the Nabatean camp we found two coins, one of Diocletian and another of Constantine I, in a trench made in antiquity by the laborers who were employed to dismantle the south wall of the camp; the coins helped in dating the time of construction of the new citadel.
95. *Nessana* I, pp. 16–18, 31–32; pls. LXII, LXVI.
96. See, e.g., M. Avi-Yonah in *EAEHL* III, 1977, p. 292: "The fort was built for stationing the Theodosian Numerus—'the most loyal.'"
97. *Nessana* III, index VII, official and military terms, p. 342.
98. *Nessana* III, no. 15, pp. 41–44, reads: "Rhinocorura City. May 30, 512 (C.E.). This written document has been executed voluntarily and without compulsion. Flavius Stephan son of Abraham, soldier in the regiment of the Very Loyal

Theodosians, to his blood brother Aws, also a soldier in the said regiment, both natives of Nessana Village a long time ago and presently residing here in Rhinocorura. Greeting . . ."

99. See *Nessana* I, p. 7: "As Kraemer pointed out (1958.16), the unit was probably activated in the first half of the fifth century A.D., which is also the most likely date for the erection of the fort."

100. Christianity's penetration of the Negev, a fascinating chapter in itself, will not be dealt with here. My views concerning this matter are summarized in Negev, 1981d, pp. 26 ff.; Negev, 1982b, p. 306; Negev, 1983, pp. 159 ff.

101. Todd in Woolley and Lawrence, no. 11, pp. 138–139, of 426 C.E., and some undated inscriptions that are most probably pagan.

102. Negev, 1981a, no. 92, pp. 73–76.

103. The first number is the number in PNNR, index C; the second is the number in the general list of Nabatean names: 2060, 2061/791.

104. 2062, 2063, 2064/791; one was a decurio in the army.

105. 2069, 2077, 2078, 2079, 2080/510; one soldier, one adjutant, and several ordinary citizens of Nessana, Oboda, and Ruheibah.

106. 2084, 2085/451; ten citizens of Nessana, and one from Elusa.

107. 2098, 2099/452/453; from Nessana, Ruheibah, Oboda.

108. 2102/108.

109. 2106/98 or 916.

110. 2107, 2110/924; numerous people from Nessana, one of whom was a soldier.

111. 2122/854.

112. 2116/152.

113. 2120/52; a soldier from Nessana.

114. 3001; more than forty persons, from almost all the towns.

115. 3002.

116. 3004.

117. 3007; five persons.

118. 3009; nine persons.

119. 3021; twenty-four persons.

120. 3031; fifty persons.

121. 3056; six persons.

122. 2069.

123. 2073.

124. 2084.

125. 2085.

126. 2095.

127. 2101.

128. 2120.

129. 2124.

130. 3010.

131. 3021.

132. 3034.

133. 3059.

134. 3012.

135. 3019.

136. 3020.

137. 3021.

138. 3028.

139. 3029.

140. *Nessana* III, no. 80, p. 234.

141. *Nessana* III, nos. 90, 91, pp. 261–289.

142. 2506.

143. 2507.

144. 2508.

145. 2509.

146. 2510.

147. 2538.

148. 2645–2702.

149. The Nabatean and the Greco-Nabatean inscriptions at Oboda have already been alluded to several times; at Nessana nine Nabatean inscriptions—four on stone and five on ostraca—were found in the dump east of the North Church, originating with all probability in the Nabatean fort that underlies the church. These inscriptions contain lists of persons, possibly laborers. One, no. 4, lists a watchman and a supervisor; another ostracon, no. 5, mentions either "milk" or a personal name. See F. Rosenthal in *Nessana* I, pp. 198–210. Without supporting evidence Rosenthal dates these inscriptions to the period between 150 and 350 C.E. The early Nabatean inscription of Elusa has also been mentioned. The paucity of Nabatean and other pre-Byzantine inscriptions on the two latter sites may be explained by the limited scope of reseraches carried out on these sites.

140

It is only natural that a large number of dedicatory inscriptions would be found in a temple built by public authorities with the financial help of numerous persons.

150. See Negev, 1981c, fig. 5 on p. 590.
151. Shown to me by the excavator, Prof. Tzafrir.
152. In fact, this was the situation throughout the Nabatean realm; older temples were rebuilt, and not a single new temple was built in the second century C.E.
153. There are large waterworks in the major wadis south of Sobata, but the system of collection of water for drinking has not been investigated. See Evenari, *Negev*, pp. 110 ff.
154. See ibid., fig. 102.
155. Negev, 1982b, figs. 5, 7, 8, 10.
156. Negev, 1981b, passim.
157. Negev, 1981b, figs. 9, 22.
158. See Negev, 1981b, fig. 36, p. 28; Negev, 1983, plan on pp. 188–189, for a typical house of the Byzantine period at Oboda.
159. Negev, 1981b, fig. 26, p. 18.
160. Negev, 1981d, fig. 67.
161. Negev, 1983, pp. 183–184.
162. *Nessana* I, pl. XVII.
163. *Nessana* I, pl. XV, 3.
164. Rosenthal, 1982, pls. 49a, b; 56a, b.
165. Negev, 1982b, fig. 31, p. 23.
166. See Negev, 1974a, for the capitals from Oboda, Mampsis, and Elusa; and see *Nessana* I, pl. XIX, 4, for a small capital of this type from Nessana.
167. Negev, 1974a, pl. 27d, e, f.
168. Negev, 1974a, pl. 27c.
169. Negev, 1974a, pl. 28b, c.
170. Negev, 1974a, pl. 28e.
171. At Nessana: *Nessana* I, pls. XV, 6, around a cross; pl. XVII, 4, at the base of a capital; pl. XVII, 8, at the base of a doorpost capital; at Sobata: Rosenthal, 1982, pl. 55a, a doorpost base; pl. 58a, crudely made, on a lintel; pl. 61c, around a cross; pl. 63a, doorpost capital; Oboda: Negev, 1981d, fig. 31b, a lintel, and on numerous other architectural stones at Oboda and Mampsis,

about which nothing has been published.
172. Negev, 1974a, pl. 28a, b.
173. Negev, 1974a, pl. 28f.
174. Unpublished.
175. Negev, 1974a, pl. 29d.
176. Oboda: Wiegand, *Sinai*, fig. 88r, on a doorpost capital, and on other stones unpublished as yet; *Nessana* I, pl. XVII, 7, a doorpost capital, probably with a cross; Wiegand, *Sinai*, fig. 106, p. 104, doorpost capital with a cross, fig. 111, p. 108; Sobata: Rosenthal, 1982, pl. 50c, on a lintel, at the sides of a wreath containing a cross; pl. 51a, b, doorpost capitals; pl. 65b, doorpost capital, schematically made; pl. 66b, doorpost capital; Wiegand, *Sinai*, fig. 71, p. 77, doorpost capital; fig. 76, p. 80, doorpost capital; Ruheibah: fig. 47, p. 59, doorpost capital.
177. Negev, 1983, p. 81; Wiegand, *Sinai*, fig. 88i, p. 91.
178. Negev, 1974b, pls. 4–6, 13.
179. Negev, 1983, p. 140; p. 141, bottom right.
180. Nessana: Wiegand, *Sinai*, fig. 111, p. 108, four doorpost capitals; *Nessana* I, pl. XV, 4, forming a wreath around a cross; pl. XVI, 3, doorpost capital with a cross in the middle; Sobata: Rosenthal, 1982, pls. 63a, b; 65d, doorpost capitals.
181. Negev, 1974b, pl. 11, 34, and the late bowl shown on pl. 12, 36.
182. Negev, 1983, especially the earring on p. 148.
183. See, e.g., Glueck, *DD*, pls. 30a, 134a; and see index, p. 641, "grapes"; p. 641, "wine." Glueck seems to have overemphasized the importance of these two pieces of sculpture, the only ones with grapes on the site. Of all of the Greco-Roman gods represented at Khirbet et-Tannur it is Dionysus who is missing from his repertoire. In any case, the art of Khirbet et-Tannur still stands isolated in Nabatean iconography, and its place has not yet been satisfactorily explained in an art that is basically uniconic. See Patrich, 1983.

Patrich also devoted his M.A. thesis to the subject of the uniconic tendency in Nabatean art.

184. Negev, 1983, pp. 208–214. I am deliberately avoiding the ambiguous problem of the Tuleilat el-Anab, the "mounds of grapes."

185. Mazor, 1981.

186. *Nessana* III, nos. 16, 31, 34, 97, but wine itself is not mentioned in these documents.

187. Rosenthal, 1982, pl. 51c, on a lintel; pl. 71a, on a lintel.

188. *Nessana* I, pl. XIX, 1.

189. Negev, 1981d, fig. 48, p. 31, on the right side of the chancel screen, and also on a chancel screen from the North Church.

190. Negev, 1983, p. 174, on the mosaic pavement.

191. *Nessana* III, PC 58–59, pp. 168–174.

192. *Nessana* III, PC 60, 61, 62, 63, 64, 65, 66, 67, pp. 180–197.

193. *Nessana* III, PC 69, pp. 199–201.

194. *Nessana* III, PC 70, pp. 202–203.

195. *Nessana* III, PC 72, 73, pp. 205–208.

196. *Nessana* III, PC 74, pp. 209–211.

197. *Nessana* III, PC 75, pp. 212–214.

Bibliography and Abbreviations

AASOR   *Annual of the American Schools of Oriental Research.*

ADAJ   *Annual of the Department of Antiquities of Jordan.*

Bachmann, *Petra*   W. Bachmann, C. Watzinger, and T. Wiengand, *Petra.* Berlin, 1921.

B-D I   R. E. Bruennow and A. von Domaszewski, *Die Provincia Arabia,* vol. 1. Strassburg, 1904.

Browning, *Petra*   I. Browning, *Petra.* London, 1974.

BSAOS   *Bulletin of the Schools of Oriental and African Studies.*

Butler, *Architecture*   H. C. Butler, *Architecture and Other Arts, Publications of an American Expedition to Syria in 1899–1900,* part II. New York, 1903.

Butler, *PPAES*   H. C. Butler, *Publications of the Princeton Archaeological Expeditions to Syria in 1904–1905, and 1909.* Leiden, 1919.

Cantineau I, II   J. Cantineau, *Le Nabatéen.* Paris, 1930, 1932.

CIS II   *Corpus inscriptionum semiticarum. Pars secunda, inscriptiones aramicas continens.* II.1. Paris, 1907.

Dalman, 1908   G. Dalmann, *Petra und seine Felsheiligtuemer.* Leipzig, 1908.

Dalman, *NPF*   ———, *Neue Petra Forschungen.* Leipzig, 1912.

Doe, *South Arabia*   B. Doe, *South Arabia.* London, 1971.

EAEHL   *Encyclopedia of Archaeological Excavations in the Holy Land.* Oxford University Press, vols. I–IV, 1973–1978.

EB 1–8   *Encyclopaedia Biblica.* Jerusalem, 1955–1982 (Hebrew).

EI   *Eretz-Israel, Archaeological, Historical and Geographical Studies*. Hebrew, English summaries.

Eissfeldt, 1969   O. Eissfeldt, "Neue Belege fuer nabateische kultgenossenschaften." *Mitteilungen des Instituts fuer Orientforschung* 15 (1969): 217–227.

Euting, 1891   J. Euting, *Sinaitische Inschriften*. Berlin, 1891.

Evenari, *Negev*   M. Evenari, L. Shanan, and N. Tadmor, *The Negev: The Challenge of a Desert*. Harvard College, 1971.

Glueck, *DD*   N. Glueck, *Deities and Dolphins: The Story of the Nabateans*. New York, 1951.

Hammond, 1977/78   P. C. Hammond, "Excavations at Petra 1975–1977." *ADAJ* 22 (1977–1978): 81–107.

Hornblower, 1981   J. Hornblower, *Hieronymus of Cardia*. Oxford University Press, 1981.

Horsfield, 1938, 1939, 1942   G. and A. Horsfield, "Sela-Petra: The Rock, of Edom and Nabatene." *QDAP* 7 (1938); 8 (1939); 9 (1942).

ICPAN   G. L. Harding, *An Index and Concordance of Pre-Islamic Arabian Names and Inscriptions*. Toronto, 1971.

IEJ   *Israel Exploration Journal*.

Jaussen-Savignac, *Mission* I, II   A. Jaussen and R. Savignac, *Mission archéologique en Arabie*, I, II. Paris, 1909, 1914.

Jaussen-Vincent-Savignac, 1904   A. Jaussen, H. Vincent, and R. Savignac, "Abdéh (4–9 février 1904)." *RB* 13 (1904): 403–424; 14 (1905): 74–89, 279–298.

Kammerer, *Petra*   A. Kammerer, *Pétra et la Nabatène*. Paris, 1929.

Littman and Meredith, 1953, 1954   E. Littman and D. Meredith, "Nabatean Inscriptions from Egypt." *BSOAS* [University of London] 15 (1953): 1–27; 16 (1954): 211–246.

Mazor, 1981   G. Mazor, "The Wine-Press in the Negev." *Qadmoniot* 14 (1981): 51–60 (Hebrew).

Meshorer, *Coins*   Y. Meshorer, *Nabatean Coins, Qedem 3, Monographs of the Institute of Archaeology*. The Hebrew University of Jerusalem, 1975.

Meyers, *Ossuaries*   E. M. Meyers, *Jewish Ossuaries. Secondary Burials in Their Near Eastern Setting*. Rome, 1971; and see A. Negev, review article in *Journal of Jewish Studies* 25 (1974): 337–342.

Milik and Starcky, 1975   J. T. Milik and J. Starcky, "Inscriptions recement découverts à Pétra." *ADAJ* 20 (1975): 111–130.

Moritz, 1916   B. Moritz, *Sinaikult in heidnischer Zeit*. Berlin, 1916.

Murray and Ellis   M. A. Murray and J. C. Ellis, *A Street in Petra.* London, 1940.

Naveh, 1970   J. Naveh, "Sinaitic Remarks." *Sepher Shemuel Yeivin.* Jerusalem, 1970. Pp. 371–374 (Hebrew).

Negev, 1961   A. Negev, "Nabatean Inscriptions from Avdat (Oboda)." *IEJ* 11 (1961): 113–118.

Negev, 1963   ———, "Nabatean Inscriptions from Avdat (Oboda)." II, *IEJ* 13 (1963): 117–122.

Negev, 1966   ———, "The Date of the Petra–Gaza Road." *PEQ* 99 (1966): 89–98.

Negev, 1967a   ———, "Oboda, Mampsis and the Provincia Arabia." *IEJ* 17 (1967): 46–55.

Negev, 1967b   ———, "New Dated Nabatean Graffiti from the Sinai." *IEJ* 17 (1967): 250–255.

Negev, 1969a   ———, "Seal Impressions from Tomb 107 at Kurnub (Mampsis)." *IEJ* 19 (1969): 89–106.

Negev, 1969b   ———, "The Chronology of the Middle Nabatean Period." *PEQ* 101 (1969): 5–14.

Negev, 1971   ———, "The Nabatean Necropolis of Mampsis (Kurnub)." *IEJ* 21 (1971): 110–129.

Negev, 1971a   ———, "New Graffiti from Sinai." *EI* 10 (1971): 183–184 (Hebrew).

Negev, 1973   ———, "The Staircase-Tower in Nabatean Architecture." *RB* 80 (1973): 364–383.

Negev, 1974a   ———, "Nabatean Capitals from the Towns of the Negev." *IEJ* 24 (1974): 153–159.

Negev, 1974b   ———, *The Nabatean Potter's Workshop at Oboda.* Bonn, 1974.

Negev, 1976a   ———, "The Early Beginnings of the Nabatean Realm." *PEQ* 108, pp. 125–133.

Negev, 1976b   ———, "The Nabatean Necropolis at Egra." *RB* 83 (1976): 203–236.

Negev, 1976c   ———, "Survey and Trial Excavations at Halusa (Elusa)." *IEJ* 26 (1976): 89–95.

Negev, 1977a   ———, *The Inscriptions of Wadi Haggag, Sinai, Qedem 6, Monographs of the Institute of Archaeology.* The Hebrew University, Jerusalem, 1977.

Negev, 1977b   ———, "A Nabatean Sanctuary at Jebel Moneijah, Southern Sinai." *IEJ* 27 (1977): 219–231.

Negev, 1977c   ———, "The Nabateans and the Provincia Arabia," in H. Temporini and W. Haase, *Aufstieg und Niedergang der Roemischen Welt*. II, 8. Berlin and New York, 1977. Pp. 520–586.

Negev, 1977d ———, "Excavations at Avdat 1975–1976." *Qadmoniot* 10 (1977): 27–29 (Hebrew).

Negev, 1978 ———, "Characmoba Seal-Impressions from Mampsis" (pp. 110–112); "Petra Seal-Impessions from Mampsis" (pp. 236–239); "Rabbathmoba Seal-Impressions from Mampsis" (pp. 274–276), in A. Spijkerman, *The Coins of the Decapolis and Provincia Arabia*. Jerusalem, 1978.

Negev, 1980 ———, "House and City Planning in the Ancient Negev and the Provincia Arabia," in G. Golani, ed., *Housing in Arid Lands: Design and Planning*. London and New York, 1980. Pp. 5–32.

Negev, 1980a ———, "The Inscriptions of Southern Sinai," in Z. Meshel and I. Finkelstein, eds., *Sinai in Antiquity: Researches in the History and Archaeology of the Peninsula*. Tel Aviv, 1980. Pp. 333–378 (Hebrew).

Negev, 1981a ———, *The Greek Inscriptions from the Negev*. Jerusalem, 1981.

Negev, 1981b ———, "Nabatean, Greek and Thamudic Inscriptions from the Wadi Haggag–Jebel Musa Road." *IEJ* 31 (1981): 66–71.

Negev, 1981c ———, "Elusa (1980)." *RB* 88 (1981): 589–591.

Negev, 1981d ———, "Nabatéens et Byzantins au Negev." *Le Monde de la Bible* 19 (1981): 4–46.

Negev, 1982a ———, "Numismatics and Nabatean Chronology." *PEQ* 114 (1982): 119–127.

Negev, 1982b ———, "Christen und Christentum in der Wueste Negev." *Antike Welt* 13 (1982): 2–33.

Negev, 1983 ———, *Tempel, Kirchen und Zisternen*. Stuttgart, 1983.

Negev, 1986 ———, *The Late Hellenistic and Early Roman Pottery of Oboda*. Jerusalem, 1986.

Negev, PNNR ———, "Personal Names in the Nabatean Realm." Work in progress.

Negev-Sivan, 1977 A. Negev and R. Sivan, "The Pottery of the Nabatean Necropolis at Mampsis." *RCRF, Acta* 17/18 (1977): 119–131.

Nessana I H. D. Colt, ed., *Excavations at Nessana*, vol. 1. London, 1962.

146

Nessana III   C. C. Kraemer, Jr., *Excavations at Nessana, Vol. 3, Non-Literary Papyri.* Princeton, N.J., 1958. (PC refers to number of papyri in the collection.)

Parr, Sequence   P. J. Parr, "A Sequence of Pottery from Petra," in J. A. Sanders, ed., *Essays in Honor of Nelson Glueck, Near Eastern Archeology in the Twentieth Century.* New York, 1970. Pp. 348–381.

Patrich, 1983   Y. Patrich, "Earrings of the Goddess El-Uzza from Mampsis." *Qadmoniot* 16 (1983): 86–88 (Hebrew).

PEF Annual   *Annual of the Palestine Exploration Fund.*

PEQ   *Palestine Exploration Quarterly.*

QDAP   *Quarterly of the Department of Antiquities of Palestine.*

RB   *Revue Biblique.*

RCRF   *Rei Cretariae Romanae Fautorum.*

RES   Répertoire d'Epigraphie sémitique. Paris, 1907–1914.

Rosenthal, 1970   R. Rosenthal, "Die Goldschmuck von Mampsis und Oboda," in *Die Nabataeer.* Munich, 1970.

Rosenthal, 1982   R. Rosenthal-Heginbottom, *Die Kirchen von Sobota und die Dreiapsidenkirchen des Nahen Osten.* Wiesbaden, 1982.

Savignac, 1933   R. Savignac, "Le Sanctuaire d'Allat a Iram." *RB* 42 (1933): 405–422.

Savignac-Horsfield, 1935   R. Savignac and G. Horsfield, "Le Temple de Ramm." *RB* 44 (1935): 245–278.

Starcky, *Dictionnaire*   J. Starcky, *Dictionnaire de la Bible,* Supplement 7. Paris, 1966, cols. 886–1017.

Starcky, *Histoire*   ———, *Histoire des Religions,* vol. 4. Paris, 1971.

Stark, 1971   J. K. Stark, *Personal Names in Palmyrene Inscriptions.* Oxford, 1971.

Steph. Byz.   Stephan von Byzanz, *Ethnika,* ed. A. Meineke. Reprint Graz, 1958.

Tushingham, *Dibon*   A. D. Tushingham, "The Excavations at Dibon (Dhiban) in Moab, The Third Campaign." *AASOR* 40 (1972).

Wiegand, *Petra*   T. Wiegand, Berlin and Leipsig, 1920.

Wiegand, *Sinai*   T. Wiegand, *Sinai.* Berlin and Leipzig, 1920.

Winnett and Reed, 1970   F. W. Winnett and W. L. Reed, *Ancient Records from North Arabia.* University of Toronto Press, 1970.

Woolley and Lawrence   C. L. Woolley and T. E. Lawrence, "The Wilderness of Zin," *PEF Annual* 3 (1914–1915).

Wright, 1969   G. R. H. Wright, "Strabo on Funerary Customs at Petra." *PEQ* 101 (1969): 113–116.

Wuthnow   H. Wuthnow, *Die Semitischen Menschennamen und Papyri des vorderen Orients.* Leipzig, 1930.

Yadin, 1962   Y. Yadin, "The Expedition to the Judean Desert, 1961, Expedition D—The Cave of the Letters." *IEJ* 12 (1962): 227–257.

Yadin, 1965   ———, "The Excavations at Masada 1963/64." *IEJ* 15 (1965): 1–115.

Postscript

In the later steps of my work on the PNNR undertaken very recently at the Institute for Advanced Study my uneasiness with the Nabatean inscriptions, on which this work is based, has been growing. These inscriptions are religious in nature, engraved by pilgrims visiting religious centers. The detailed funerary texts do not express grief, but are rather legal documents. None of the Nabatean-Aramaic inscriptions, of which there are many thousands, refer to love, hate, war, or any other human activity, and only by a meticulous study of personal names is any glimpse obtained into the daily life of the Nabateans. We have in fact learned little about the internal organization of this people from these inscriptions. We know nothing of the tribes and clans. Only royalty, military, and temple administration come to the foreground. Judging by the Nabatean system of names, one can, however, see that this is a mixed society, with a rather large percentage of people with foreign personal names.

Now, in about the same geographical region and distinct from the Nabatean inscriptions, there are some 15,000 written records, in an Arabic dialect, a script derived from one of the sophisticated south Arabian alphabets. These contain more than 5000 personal names, as against 1,263 personal names recorded in the Nabatean inscriptions. Unlike the Nabatean inscriptions, few of these are of a religious nature; most allude to daily life. Many speak of love, grief, war (some even refer to wars of the Nabateans, events never mentioned in the Nabateans' own inscriptions). They speak of the digging of wells, the disappointment of not finding water, the looking after of animals, the hunt, and other aspects of daily life. There are also many references to tribes and clans. In the Nabatean inscriptions there are no such references.

These particular inscriptions, which were discovered in the middle of the eighteenth century in the deserts of the northern Arabia, Jordan, and the Syro-Iraqi desert, were named "Safaitic" inscriptions, after the region. Only a few were found in the Negev and in the Southern Sinai. There seems a correlation between the decline of the Nabatean-Aramaic script and the rise of the "Safaitic" script. On the one hand, in areas where by the end of the first century C.E. the Nabatean-Aramaic script dwindles, the "Safaitic" inscriptions increase. On the other hand, in the Negev and especially in Sinai, where Nabatean-Aramaic was in use until the very end of the third century, the "Safaitic" inscriptions are rare.

Looking at these facts, I am going to suggest that the so-called "Safaitic" inscriptions are not the product of anonymous Arab tribes, but rather are the records of the Nabateans themselves. The discovery of the Nabatean-Arabic bilingual inscription at Oboda only confirms the well-known fact that the Nabateans did indeed speak Arabic "at home." Would it not be strange that a people who knew how to write from early times would not make records in their own language? I suggest it would be strange, and I suggest that the Nabatean-Aramaic and the "Safaitic" inscriptions ought themselves to be treated as two components of the same human phenomenon, and that once fitted together as two unequal parts of the same bowl, they shed new light on the Nabatean culture as a whole. This, I believe, is the duty of the Nabatean archaeologists of tomorrow.

Institute for Advanced Study
Princeton, NJ
June 1986

Index

DATE DUE

7 1991			
7 1991			
JAN 7 1991			
FEB 1 8 1991			